From the Galleys of

Women Aboard

A collection of tips and recipes
from the Sea Sisters
of Women Aboard, 1994-2001

Compiled and edited by Maria Russell

Published by **WOMEN ABOARD**® Printed in the United States of America

Cover design by Dave Russell.

ISBN 0-9663520-2-5

Questions regarding the ordering of this book should be addressed to:
Seaworthy Publications, Inc.
215 S. Park St., Ste. #1
Port Washington, WI 53074
U.S.A.
262-268-9250
www.seaworthy.com

For more information regarding THE Network for Women in Boating:
WOMEN ABOARD
P.O. Box 14254
North Palm Beach, FL 33408
U.S.A.
877-WMN-ABRD
www.womenaboard.com

WOMEN ABOARD®
is an organization dedicated to empowering women boaters.

What began with a handful of women in 1994 has evolved into an
international networking group of thousands of Sea Sisters.
Our goal is to enhance the boating experience for all women in boating
through information, education, camaraderie and support.

Our newsletter is the cornerstone of our network. It provides a
supportive forum enabling members to ask questions and seek advice. It
contains personal accounts of experiences and adventures.

This cookbook is a compilation of recipes and tips contributed by
the Sea Sisters of **WOMEN ABOARD®** from 1994-2001.
We are grateful to them for sharing these with us, for without them
this cookbook would not have been possible.

I'm also grateful to these special people:

Our publisher, Joe Janson, for his guidance, friendship, and patience.
My friend, Carin Johnson, our "Gal Friday," whose help enabled me to
focus on this book and work for hours uninterrupted.
And most especially my husband, Dave, who always has there behind the
scenes. I couldn't do what I do without him.

Maria Russell, Founder
October 2001

Contributors to
From the Galleys of Women Aboard

Nancy Abramson
Marcia Alley
Elizabeth Bagur
Pat Block
Cindy Roepke Breeding
Joyce Brownell
Susan Campbell
Linda Carter
Mary Ann Chapman
Betsy Dockman
Mary Jane Douglass
Dottye Ellis
June Francis
Gwen Fraser
Peggy Glass
Anne Gould
Mary Frances Graham
Tena Deuel Grisham
Cher Hill
Patti Hutto
Daily Juneau
Denise Keary
Sandy Larsen
Carol Lawrence

Sue Longacre
Jane Mick
Anne Monnier
Jacki Timmons-Moraski
Joan Nubie
Lynn McFayden O'Connell
Susan Parr
Chris Pope
Pat Poupore
Sherry Schie
Carol Schoeman
Virginia Shell
Millie Simmonis
Anita Simmons
Jeanette Skillings
Lou Ann Riske Smith
Robin Slaughter
Judy Snow
Mary Lou Van Teylingen
Laura Wenslaff
Ann Wilson
Sallye Woodward
Judy Zegke

Credits:
Page 9, excerpt taken from The Wind in the Willows, by Kenneth Grahame,
copyright 1908. Illustration by Elaine Williams.

From the Galleys of Women Aboard

Table of Contents

BELIEVE ME, MY YOUNG FRIEND, (SAID THE WATER RAT

SOLEMNLY), THERE IS NOTHING---ABSOLUTELY NOTHING---

HALF SO MUCH WORTH DOING AS SIMPLY MESSING AROUND

IN BOATS. SIMPLY MESSING.....NOTHING SEEMS REALLY TO

MATTER, THAT'S THE CHARM OF IT. WHETHER YOU GET AWAY,

OR WHETHER YOU DON'T; WHETHER YOU ARRIVE AT YOUR

DESTINATION OR WHETHER YOU REACH SOMEWHERE ELSE, OR

WHETHER YOU NEVER GET ANYWHERE AT ALL, YOU'RE ALWAYS

BUSY. AND YOU NEVER DO ANYTHING IN PARTICULAR........

---THE WIND IN THE WILLOWS

TROPICAL DELIGHT

1 can mandarin oranges, drained
1 can chunk pineapple, drained
1 banana, sliced
1 Tbsp. coconut
2 cups plain yogurt

Mix all ingredients except coconut. Serve in champagne glasses with a sprinkle of coconut on top. Makes a great no-fat dessert or breakfast fruit dish.

HOT MULLED CIDER

1/2 gallon of fresh cider
5 cinnamon sticks
10 whole cloves
4 round slices of orange
1/4 cup of brown sugar

Put all ingredients, except orange slices, in a crock pot and heat on high until hot. Add orange slices and squeeze juice out of leftover part of orange into pot. Leave crock pot on warm so crew can have refills all morning. Serve cider in mugs, with a dusting of nutmeg on each serving.

HOT AND SPICY TOMATO WARMER

1 cup V-8 juice
1 beef bouillon cube

Heat until bouillon cube melts. Serve in mug. Hot, satisfying, and quick!

For Starters: Beverages, Appetizers, and Snacks

HOT BUTTERED RUM
Guaranteed to warm your soul on cold, damp nights.

1/4 cup dark rum
Cinnamon stick
Twist of lemon peel
2 cloves
1 bottle cider
1 Tbsp. unsalted butter
Sugar
Nutmeg

Put the rum, cinnamon, lemon peel, and cloves into a large mug. Heat the cider until it boils. Pour into mug. Add butter and stir; sugar to taste. Sprinkle with nutmeg.

Beverage Tips:

Cafe mocha at half the cost: Add 1/2 envelope of instant cocoa mix to one cup of strong black coffee.

For a special coffee flavor: Put a piece of chocolate or a vanilla bean in the coffee filter before you add the coffee.

Just a little honey left at the bottom of the jar? Add a cup of boiling water to the jar, then your favorite tea bag. Let is steep and treat yourself to a relaxing break.

For a creamier coffee creamer, simply add a teaspoon of nonfat dry milk.

To keep beverages warmer longer, serve them in a crock-pot. Stabilize the crock pot while underway by setting inside galley sink.

GOOD GLOP DIP

2 cups shredded cheddar cheese
3 green onions, chopped
8 slices bacon (fried crisp and crumbled)
1/4 cup slivered almonds
Mayonnaise – enough to mix

Combine all ingredients in a bowl; refrigerate for 24 hours. Add more mayonnaise if necessary when ready to serve. Use as a dip for crackers or large Fritos.

FINGER-LICKING CAESAR CRUNCHIES

Combine in bowl and mix together:
1 package dry Caesar salad dressing mix
3/4 cup olive oil
1 heaping tsp. of each: dill, onion powder, lemon-pepper
Pinch of each to taste: red pepper, cumin powder, garlic powder

Add:
1 12-oz. package oyster crackers

Stir carefully with a wooden spoon until crackers are coated and serve. It's hard to stop with just one nibble.

A large cup hook hung by the galley sink makes a handy holder for rings, watches, and bracelets while you're doing the dishes.

If sprayed with spray starch, pot holders will stay clean longer.

PINWHEELS

2 8-oz. packages cream cheese, softened
1 package ranch dressing mix
2 green onions, minced
4 12" flour tortillas
1 4-oz. jar diced pimientos, rinsed and drained
1 4-oz. can diced green chilies, rinsed and drained
1 2-oz. can sliced ripe olives, rinsed and drained

Mix cream cheese, salad dressing mix, and onions until blended. Spread on tortillas. Sprinkle dry pimientos, chilies, and olives over cream cheese mixture.

Roll tortillas up tightly. Wrap each tortilla individually in plastic wrap. Chill at least 2 hours.

Unwrap tortillas and cut into 1" pieces. Discard ends. Serve with spirals facing up. Makes 3 dozen appetizers.

PIZZA ON A PITA

3 whole wheat pitas
4 oz. mozzarella cheese
1 tsp. vegetable oil
1 small jar or can of pizza sauce
Pepperoni or other toppings of your choice

Cut pitas in half by separating at the edges to make two pizza crusts out of each pita. Top pita halves with pizza sauce, cheese, and toppings. Fry in oil until crust is lightly browned.

FLOUR TORTILLAS

4 cups flour
1 1/2 tsp. salt
1/2 cup shortening
1 1/4 cups warm water

In a mixing bowl, mix flour and salt. Cut shortening into flour and add small amounts of water while mixing. Form into a dough and knead thoroughly. Dough should be smooth and elastic. Form 18 dough balls. Sprinkle dough with flour to keep from sticking. Keep dough covered while making tortillas.

Heat griddle, but do not grease. Take a dough ball and make a circle using your hands. With your fingers, make small indentations all around the circle. With a rolling pin, flatten dough to make a 12" circle. Place on griddle until bubbles form. Flip and cook other side. Turn only once. Place hot tortillas in a bowl or store in an air-tight container and cover. Keep in a cool, dry place. Makes 18 tortillas.

Did you know that tortillas stored at room temperature will keep for almost a month, and as long as four months if kept cold?

Need a substitute for fresh cilantro? One Sea Sister swears by bottled Recaito®, by Goya, found in the Mexican food aisle. For a quick salsa, try Rotel® tomatoes, chopped onion, and Recaito®.

HOMEMADE TORTILLAS

2 cups corn flour
3/4 tsp. salt
1 cup water (plus a little more, if necessary)

In a bowl, combine flour and salt and mix well. Add water, a little at a time, while mixing. Take dough in hands and form into an elastic dough. Knead thoroughly. If necessary, add more water to keep the dough moist. Dough should hold its shape, but still be moist.

Form 12 dough balls. Take 2 sheets of waxed paper and place one dough ball in the center. Using a small plate, press down and flatten the dough. Make a thin tortilla, 6" in diameter. Cook on an ungreased griddle, leaving the top sheet of waxed paper on the tortilla. Cook until the edges of the tortilla turn brown and small air bubbles stop forming. Remove second sheet of waxed paper, flip tortilla, and cook other side. Do the same with all dough balls.

Allow tortillas to cool; then place in a plastic bag and refrigerate. Makes 12.

<u>To make chips</u>
Fried: Cut corn tortillas into quarters. Fry until crisp and drain on paper towels. Salt to taste.

Baked: Dip whole corn tortilla into water; cut into quarters. Place single layer on baking sheet. Bake at 450° approximately 6 minutes, turning midway. Salt to taste.

EASY CON QUESO DIP

1 10-oz. package frozen chopped spinach, thawed
1 2-oz. jar diced pimento, drained
1 lb. Velveeta cheese with jalapeño peppers, cubed
1 medium tomato, diced
1/4 cup minced onion
1/2 cup skim milk

Place spinach between paper towels and squeeze until barely moist. Set aside. Combine cheese, milk, onion, and pimento in top of double-boiler; bring water to boil. Reduce heat to low; cook until cheese melts. Add spinach and tomato, stirring well.

Serve with warm tortilla chips. Makes 2 cups.

THE BIG DIPPER

1 15-oz. can Hormel chili without beans
1 10-oz. can Rotel tomatoes and green chilies, diced (drain, reserving 1 Tbsp. for garnish)
1 1/2 cups (approx. 8 oz.) Velveeta cheese, cubed
1/2 cup sliced green onions
1/2 tsp. cayenne pepper

In saucepan, combine all ingredients. Heat slowly just until cheese melts, stirring frequently. Garnish dip with reserved tomatoes, red pepper, and additional green onion, if desired.

Serve warm with assorted raw vegetable dippers and toasted French bread slices or tostado chips.

MEXICAN TUNA DIP

2 cans of tuna, chilled
1 Tbsp. of mayonnaise or Miracle Whip
1/4 cup chopped spring onions
1/4 cup salsa
3 Tbsp. hot sauce

Mix all of the above ingredients and chill. Serve with Doritos.

MEXICAN APPETIZER

16 medium flour tortillas
1 cup chopped onion
1 can chopped green chilies, drained
Garlic salt or garlic powder, to taste
8 oz. low-fat cottage cheese
8 oz. Neufchatel cheese, softened

Put cottage cheese in blender and blend until smooth. Mix softened
Neufchatel and cottage cheeses. Mix in chilies, onion, and garlic salt or
powder. Spread mixture on tortillas. Roll tortillas in jellyroll fashion.
Chill 3-4 hours. Cut each roll into 3-5 pieces and serve with salsa.

Canned refried beans often contain lard, which is animal fat. Look for
one that says "Fat Free." It will not have lard or oil.

Brush a little oil on the grater before you start grating and cheese will
wash off the grater easily.

MEXICAN CHEESE SQUARES

2 eggs, beaten
2 Tbsp. flour
1/2 tsp. salt
1/3 cup milk
1/2 lb. sharp cheddar cheese, grated
1/2 lb. Monterrey Jack cheese, grated
1 can of green chilies

Heat oven to 350°. Mix flour, salt, milk, and eggs with electric mixer. Add cheese and chilies. Mix with spoon. Spray bottom of 8" x 10" baking pan with non-stick spray. Pour mixture into pan and bake for 35 minutes. Cool for a few minutes, then cut. If doubling the recipe, use a 9" x 12" pan.

7 LAYER SOMBRERO DIP

1 16-oz. can refried beans
1 8-oz. container sour cream
1 package ranch dressing mix
1 cup diced tomatoes
1 4-oz. can diced green chilies, rinsed and drained
3/4 cup shredded cheddar cheese
3/4 cup shredded Monterrey Jack cheese
Chopped avocado

Spread beans on 10" serving platter. Blend sour cream and salad dressing mix. Spread over beans.

Layer tomatoes, chilies, olives, and cheeses. Serve with tortilla chips.

TOO EASY CLAM DIP!

1 8-oz. package cream cheese
1 can clams, drained (reserve juice)
Dash of Worcestershire sauce

Blend cream cheese with hand mixer. Add clams and mix until smooth. Add enough of the reserved clam juice to make it dip-able. Add Worcestershire sauce to taste. Serve with your favorite chips or crackers.

This can be made ahead of time. Just be sure to thin it a little with some of the reserved clam juice.

CRABMEAT SNACK

1/2 cup ketchup
1 Tbsp. lemon juice
2 tsp. horseradish
1 8-oz. block fat-free cream cheese, softened
1/2 cup fresh crab meat or surimi (imitation crab)

Mix ketchup, lemon juice, and horseradish in a small bowl. Place block of cream cheese on a serving pate and spread the ketchup mixture over cream cheese. Top with chopped crabmeat. Serve with crackers.

Next time: Top with chopped, cooked shrimp instead of crabmeat.

For refrigerator and freezer odors, pour one of the following "odor eaters" into a saucer and place it in the refrigerator: charcoal, dried coffee grounds, vanilla bean or extract on a piece of cotton, baking soda, or crumpled newspaper.

SEAFOOD DIP

1 cup cooked shrimp or crabmeat, finely chopped
1 8-oz. container sour cream
1/4 cup chili sauce
1 package ranch dressing mix
Crackers or assorted vegetables for dipping

Combine shrimp or crabmeat, sour cream, chili sauce, and salad dressing mix in medium bowl. Refrigerate at least 1 hour before serving with crackers and vegetables. Makes about 2 cups.

CRAB CRISPS

1 6-oz. can crabmeat, drained and flaked
1 6-oz. package frozen crab, thawed, drained and flaked
1 8-oz. carton sour cream
2 Tbsp. dry onion soup mix
3 doz. Melba rounds or crackers

Combine first 4 ingredients, mixing well. Spread on crackers. Broil 4-5" from heat, 2-3 minutes.

EASY CRABMEAT DIP

1 (8 ounce) package cream cheese, softened
1 (8 ounce) jar cocktail sauce
3/4 pound imitation crab, chopped into small pieces

In a medium bowl, blend the cream cheese and cocktail sauce. Add crab. Refrigerate 3 hours before serving.

Breakfast

APPLESAUCE SPICE MUFFINS

Mix:
2 1/2 cups Kellogg's raisin bran cereal
1/4 cup skim milk
1 cup applesauce

Let stand until cereal softens, approximately 4 minutes.

Then add:
1 egg
1/4 cup vegetable oil.
Mix well.

Mix:
1 1/4 cups all-purpose flour
1/4 cup sugar
1 Tbsp. baking powder
1/4 tsp. salt
1/4 tsp. nutmeg
1/2 tsp. cinnamon

Add dry ingredients to cereal mixture. Mix well. Fill greased or muffin pan lined with paper baking cups. Bake at 400° for 20 minutes, or until done.

Make your own nonstick spray by combining equal parts of vegetable oil and liquid lecithin in a pump bottle. Liquid lecithin can be found in natural food stores.

22

Breakfast

OATMEAL-FRUIT MUFFINS

Oats, wheat germ, milk, and fruit—so many healthful ingredients in such tasty muffins!

Nonstick vegetable oil spray, or paper baking cups
1 cup all-purpose flour
3/4 cup quick OR regular rolled oats
1/3 cup toasted wheat germ
2 tsp. baking powder
1 tsp. ground cinnamon
1/2 tsp. baking soda
1/8 tsp. salt
3/4 cup fat-free milk
1/2 cup firmly packed light brown sugar
1 egg
1/4 cup unsweetened applesauce
1/2 tsp. vanilla
1/2 cup snipped dried figs or apricots (about 8 ounces figs or 3 1/2 ounces apricots)

Preheat oven to 400°. Line 12 muffin cups with paper baking cups or lightly spray with vegetable oil spray. Set aside.

In a medium bowl, stir together flour, oats, wheat germ, baking powder, cinnamon, baking soda, and salt. Make a well in the center.

In another bowl, combine remaining ingredients, except figs. Add wet mixture to dry mixture. Stir until just moistened (batter will be lumpy.) Fold in figs.

Spoon batter into muffin cups, using about 1/4 cup batter for each cup. Bake for 10-12 minutes, or until a toothpick inserted near the center comes out clean. Cool on a wire rack for 5 minutes; remove muffins from baking cups. Serve warm or at room temperature.

Breakfast

MUFFINS, OR "HOW TO WOW MR. WONDERFUL"

1 egg
3/4 cup milk
1/2 cup vegetable oil
2 cups flour
1/3 cup sugar
3 tsp. baking powder
1 tsp. salt

Heat oven to 400°. Grease bottoms only of muffin pan or line with paper baking cups. Beat egg in medium bowl; stir in milk and oil. Stir in remaining ingredients all at once just until flour is moistened (batter will be lumpy.)

Fill muffin cups about 3/4 full. Bake until golden brown, about 20 minutes. Immediately remove from pan.

Blueberry, strawberry, or raspberry muffins: Stir in 1 cup fresh or 3/4 cup frozen berries (thawed and well-drained) with the milk.

PINEAPPLE PUFFS

1/2 cup vegetable oil
1 lg. can crushed pineapple and juice
1 cup sugar
1 tsp. baking powder
1 egg
1 tsp. ground cloves
2 cups flour
1 tsp. cinnamon
1/2 tsp. baking soda

24

Breakfast

Mix everything well. Put into muffin pans. Bake until brown and tested for doneness. <u>Mini-muffins</u>: 350° for 16-18 minutes. Makes about 4 1/2 dozen tiny muffins. <u>Regular-size muffins</u>: 350° for 20-30 minutes. Makes about 12 muffins.

STICKY BUNS

Grease bundt pan with a nonstick spray. Place half of the package (about 18) of frozen dinner rolls into the bundt pan.

Cover with 1/2 package butterscotch Jell-O Cook and Serve pudding. Sprinkle with lots of cinnamon.

Melt together: 1/2 cup brown sugar, 1/2 stick butter, and 1/4 cup syrup. Then dump on top of ingredients in bundt pan.

Cover with dish towel overnight or until rolls rise. Bake at 300-350° for 30 minutes. Pull apart and serve.

THIN PANCAKES

2 eggs
1 cup milk
1/2 tsp. vanilla
3/4 cup flour
2 Tbsp. oil

Batter should be thin. Use small amount of oil in frying pan. Heat pan to moderate heat. Drop 4 Tbsp. of batter in middle of pan. Grasp handle and spread batter completely around frying pan. Cook until light brown; flip to brown other side. Wrap around prepared breakfast sausage links.

LOW-FAT, OVEN-BAKED FRENCH TOAST
Crunchy and guilt-free!

Egg Beaters equivalent to 2 eggs
2 tsp. vanilla
Nonstick vegetable oil spray
3/4 cup skim milk
1 tsp. cinnamon
6-8 slices of low-fat white or wheat bread

Preheat oven to 450°. Combine eggs, milk, vanilla, and cinnamon in a large bowl. Spray a large cookie sheet with nonstick spray. Dip bread in liquid, lightly coating each side. Place on the well-sprayed cookie sheet and bake on each side for 6-8 minutes until well browned. Flip each slice and brown the other side.

Serve with any sweet, warm fruit mixture, or make a simple fruit syrup by combining the following ingredients:

2/3 cup fruit juice
2 Tbsp. honey
1 1/2 tsp. cornstarch
1/8 tsp. cinnamon (optional)

Mix together in a small saucepan. Cook over medium heat until thick and bubbly. Serve over warm toast.

Since spices lose their punch after a while, it's a good idea to write the date that you first used the spice on the container. Discard spices after a year.

Breakfast

BLUEBERRY-ALMOND PANCAKE MIX

1 cup whole wheat flour
1/2 cup yellow cornmeal, preferably stone-ground
3 Tbsp. powdered buttermilk
2 Tbsp. powdered egg whites
1 1/2 Tbsp. granulated sugar
1 1/2 tsp. baking powder
3/4 tsp. baking soda
1/2 tsp. ground cinnamon
1/2 tsp. salt
1/2 cup dried blueberries
1/3 cup finely chopped almonds
1 Tbsp. canola oil, plus more for greasing skillet
Maple syrup (optional)
1 3/4 cups water

In an airtight plastic bag, combine all dry ingredients. Rub in 1 Tbsp. oil.
Seal bag.

When ready to eat, pour water directly into bag of pancake mix and mix
well. Let stand for 15 minutes.

Oil a nonstick skillet and heat over medium heat. Working in batches,
spoon in about 3 tablespoons of batter for each pancake. Cook until
pancakes are browned on the bottom and bubbling on top. Turn and cook
until other side is browned. Serve with maple syrup, if desired. Makes
about 16 pancakes.

These make a great snack...simply spread with a little peanut butter!

Breakfast

FIESTA BREAKFAST

1 1/2 cups frozen corn kernels, thawed
1/3 cup green pepper, diced
1/3 cup red pepper, diced
1 tsp. lemon juice
1 tsp. Old Bay seasoning
12" Boboli Italian pizza crust
5 eggs
1/2 cup sharp cheddar cheese, shredded

Preheat oven to 400°. Combine first 5 ingredients. Fill pizza crust with corn mixture, leaving a 1" border and making 5 deep indentations for each egg. Break an egg into each indentation. Sprinkle with cheese. Bake on baking sheet in lower third of oven for 12 minutes or until eggs have set. Serve immediately.

For something a little different, substitute tomatoes for the peppers.

MEXICAN BISCUIT BREAKFAST

2 - 8 oz. cans biscuits
8 oz. thick and chunky picanté sauce
1/2 cup chopped green onions
1/2 cup chopped green peppers (or use green chilies)
2-3 cups grated Monterey Jack cheese

Preheat oven to 375°. Spray 9" x 13" pan with nonstick spray.

Pour picanté sauce in large bowl. Cut each biscuit into 8 pieces and mix (toss) with picanté. Spread in prepared pan. Sprinkle with cheese, then onions and green pepper. Bake 30-40 minutes or until center is set and edges are golden brown. Let stand 15 minutes before cutting.

Breakfast

MEXICANA BRUNCH PIE

5 eggs, beaten (may use egg substitute)
2 Tbsp. Crisco, melted
1/2 cup flour
8-oz. low-fat cream-style cottage cheese
2 cups shredded cheddar or Monterey Jack cheese
4-oz. can chopped green chilies, drained

Combine first four ingredients in a mixing bowl; beat well at medium speed on electric mixer, or stir very well with whisk. Stir in remaining ingredients and pour into a well-greased 9" pie plate or quiche pan.

Bake at 400° for 10 minutes; reduce heat to 350° and bake about 20 minutes longer, or until set. Cut into wedges and serve. Makes 6 servings.

QUICK BUBBLE AND SQUEAK

1 tsp. oil
1 small onion, diced
1 cup leftover vegetables
1/2 cup cooked potatoes
1 egg white
Salt and pepper to taste

Sauté onion until golden. Add the cooked vegetables and heat through. Lower the heat and add the egg white and pepper; stir. Cook the underside of vegetables until slightly crusted. Serve with toast for a satisfying breakfast before getting underway!

EASY QUICHE LORRAINE

1 - 9" pie crust, prepared according to directions
6 slices crisp bacon
6 oz. shredded Swiss cheese
1 1/2 cups half and half
1/2 tsp. salt
1/4 tsp. nutmeg
1/2 cup ham cubes
4 eggs
1/4 cup onion, diced

Sprinkle crumbled bacon and cheese on the bottom of prepared pie crust. Put remaining ingredients in a blender. Blend on high for 10 seconds; blend until onion is mixed but do not over blend. Pour into pie crust over bacon and cheese. Bake in preheated oven at 350° for 30 minutes, until top is golden brown and mixture is set. Serve warm.

How to cook a perfect hard-cooked egg: Place egg(s) in a pot, cover with cold tap water, and bring the water to a boil over high heat. Once the water is boiling, turn the heat off, leaving the pot in place. Allow the egg to cook for 17 minutes. Cool the egg(s) by placing it in a bowl of cold tap water for 5 minutes, then peel and serve. The egg will be perfectly cooked, without the ugly dark ring caused by the separation of sulfur from the egg yolk when the egg is overcooked or not cooked quickly enough.

To code hard-cooked eggs so that they are distinguishable from the raw ones, just add a few yellow onion skins to the water while simmering; they will color the shells.

Breakfast

CHERRY-WALNUT COUSCOUS PUDDING MIX
This sweet, nutty porridge can be served for breakfast or dessert.

1/2 cup instant couscous
1/2 cup nonfat dried milk
1/4 cup dried cherries or dried cranberries
1/4 cup walnuts, finely chopped
3 Tbsp. light brown sugar
1/8 tsp. salt
1 1/4 cups water

At home or on the dock, combine all ingredients, except water, in an airtight plastic bag. Seal bag.

When ready to eat, bring water to a boil in a medium saucepan. Stir in pudding mix, cover, and remove from heat. Let stand for 10 minutes. Stir with a fork. Serves 2.

There is really no need to rehydrate dried fruit before you add it to a recipe that requires cooking. Even the hardest dried raisins or prunes will become soft and moist when cooked in recipes that contain plenty of liquid, like custards, puddings, stuffings, and most tea breads.

Some fruits and vegetables do not store well next to each other. The ethylene gas generated during ripening can drastically shorten the life of other produce. Avoid storing these produce together:
Apples and bananas
Apples and carrots
Onion and potatoes

Breads

ENGLISH MUFFINS

1 cup warm water
1 package rapid-rise dry yeast
1 tsp. sugar
2 tsp. salt
1/4 cup oil
3 cups flour
Cornmeal

Sprinkle yeast over warm water and let sit. Thoroughly mix dry ingredients and gradually add to the bowl of water. Add oil about halfway through, mixing thoroughly.

Roll out dough about 1/3" thick, and cut into 2 1/2" circles. Sprinkle with corn meal. Let rise about 2 hours, until double in size.

"Bake" on a pre-heated griddle (a large frying pan also works well) over medium heat about 5 minutes per side.

To serve, split with fork and add butter.

BAGELS

4 1/4 to 4 3/4 cups all-purpose flour
2 packages active dry yeast
1 1/2 cups warm water (110° - 115°)
3 Tbsp. sugar
1 Tbsp. salt
1 Tbsp. sugar

In a mixing bowl, combine 1 1/2 cups of flour and the yeast. In another bowl, combine warm water, sugar, and salt. Pour over the flour mixture.

32

Beat at low speed for 30 seconds to combine. Beat an additional 3 minutes at high speed. Stir in as much of the remaining flour as you can with a spoon.

Turn out onto a lightly floured surface. Knead in enough remaining flour to make a moderately stiff dough that is smooth and elastic, about 6-7 minutes. Cover; let rest for 10 minutes.

Cut into 12 portions. Shape each into a ball, poke a hole in the center, and pull gently to make hole 1-2" in diameter. Place on a greased baking sheet. Cover and let rise 20 minutes. Broil 5 inches from heat 3-4 minutes, turning once.

Heat 1 gallon of water and the 1 tablespoon of sugar to boiling; reduce heat. Cook 4-5 bagels at a time for 7 minutes, turning once. Lift out of water and allow to drain.

Place on a baking sheet. Bake in a 375° oven for 25-30 minutes.

<u>Onion bagels</u>
Cook 1/2 cup finely chopped onion in 3 tablespoons butter until tender but not brown. Brush on top of bagels after first 15 minutes of baking.

<u>Poppy seed or sesame seed bagels</u>
Before baking, brush tops of bagels with beaten eggs; sprinkle with seeds.

Hard-to-knead dough, such as pumpernickel, whole wheat, and rye, will be easier to handle if you oil your hands a little.

To keep the bowl from slipping and sliding while mixing ingredients, place it on a folded damp towel.

CHALLAH BREAD

In a mixing bowl, whisk:
1 package yeast
3/4 cup warm water
2 Tbsp. sugar
1 Tbsp. olive oil
1 egg
1 tsp. salt
1 cup flour

With a wooden spoon, beat in 1-2 cups additional flour until a soft dough forms.

Let rise until triple in size, about 3 hours. Divide into 3 strips, braid, and pinch ends together. Brush with egg white, sprinkle with sesame seeds, and let rise for 30-45 more minutes. Bake at 350° for 30 minutes. Easy!

CRUISERS' BREAD

3 cups flour
2/3 cup quick oats
1 1/2 cups warm water
2 Tbsp. sugar
1 tsp. salt
1 package rapid rise yeast

Let yeast dissolve in water. Add to all dry ingredients. Knead about 50 times; if too sticky, add a little flour. Allow to rise in bowl for a few hours. Punch down, shape into a log, place on cookie sheet, and allow to rise again. Bake for 20-25 minutes in a pre-heated 425° oven.

Breads

NO-KNEAD BEER BREAD

3 cups self-rising flour (or Bisquick)
2-3 Tbsp. sugar
12 oz. warm beer
1 egg (optional)

Combine all ingredients and mix well. Pour into a greased and floured loaf pan. Bake at 350° for one hour.

ONION CHEESE FRYING PAN BREAD

2 medium onions, sliced
2 Tbsp. butter
1 1/4 cup flour
1 tsp. baking powder
1/2 tsp. salt
1/4 cup Parmesan cheese
3 Tbsp. shortening
1/2 cup milk (may need more)
1/2 cup grated cheese

Fry onions in butter until soft. Remove from pan. Mix dry ingredients together. Cut in shortening, add milk. Spread (sticky) dough into well-greased skillet. Sprinkle with grated cheese and top with cooked onions. Cover tightly and cook over low flame until edges are lightly browned, 25-30 minutes. Good for pot lucks!

Rise to the occasion: Use water in which potatoes have been boiled to make yeast breads moister. The texture may be coarser, but the bread lasts longer.

CANTALOUPE SOUP
Refreshing!

1 whole cantaloupe, seeded
1/2 cup white wine
2 Tbsp. honey
1 Tbsp. finely chopped fresh ginger root
1/4 cup lemon juice
1/2 cup orange juice
2 Tbsp. mint, chopped (optional)

Finely dice 1/2 cantaloupe and set aside. In small, non-corrosive pot, stir together wine, honey, and ginger. Bring to a boil, simmer 2 minutes, and set aside to steep for 10 minutes. Puree the remaining half of cantaloupe in food processor. Add white wine mix to puree and process until ginger is minced. Stir purée into diced cantaloupe. Stir in lemon juice, orange juice, and chopped mint. Cover and refrigerate a minimum of 2 hours and up to 24.

CHILLED STRAWBERRY SOUP
The fresh lime juice adds just the right touch.

3 cups sliced fresh strawberries, chilled
2 cups low-fat buttermilk
2 Tbsp. sugar
Juice from 1 lime

Place all ingredients in blender or food processor. Process until very smooth. Serve immediately. Makes 4 servings.

A nice garnish for this is fresh mint leaves.

GAZPACHO #1
Keeps well and is delicious on a hot day on the boat.

1 48-oz. can tomato juice (or use Hot & Spicy V-8 juice to kick it up!)
1 medium onion, finely chopped
2 large tomatoes, peeled and chopped
1 cucumber, peeled, seeded, and sliced
2 scallions, minced
1 clove garlic, crushed
1/4 cup chopped fresh parsley
2 Tbsp. olive oil
2 Tbsp. lime juice
2 Tbsp. red wine vinegar
1 1/2 Tbsp. lemon juice
1 tsp. dried whole tarragon
1 tsp. dried basil
1 tsp. honey
1/2 tsp. salt
1/4 tsp. pepper
1/4 tsp. ground cumin
Dash of hot sauce to taste

Combine all ingredients and chill for at least 2 hours. Yields 9 cups.

To peel many tomatoes at once, place them in an old pillowcase or onion netting bag and plunge them into a pot of boiling water for a minute. The skins slip right off.

When a recipe calls for a small quantity of juice, don't cut the lemon. Just puncture it with an ice pick, then gently squeeze. Wrap the lemon in foil and store for future use.

GAZPACHO #2

1 16-oz. can tomatoes, diced
1/2 cup green pepper
1/2 cup red pepper
1/4 cup chopped onions
1/2 cup chopped carrots
1/2 cup chopped cucumber
1/4 cup chopped parsley
1 tsp. garlic, minced
2 Tbsp. olive oil
2 Tbsp. cider vinegar
1/4 cup fresh lime juice
1/2 tsp. paprika
1/4 tsp. black pepper
1/4 tsp. cumin
1/8 tsp. cayenne
2 cups vegetable juice

Place tomatoes, cucumber, peppers, onion, carrots, celery, parsley, and garlic in food processor. Add oil, vinegar, and lime juice and purée until desired consistency. Transfer to large bowl and stir in paprika, pepper, cumin, cayenne, and juice. Blend well. Refrigerate 2-3 hours. Serves 6.

SANTA FE SOUP

Cook one (1) pound hamburger and one (1) small onion. Drain.

Then add:
1 lb. Mexican Velveeta Cheese (mild)
1 can whole kernel corn with juice
1 can diced Rotel tomatoes (mild)
1 can stewed tomatoes

2 cans ranch beans (drained)
3/4 - 1 cup milk
1/2 cup water

Mix all together and cook over low heat. (Works well in slow cooker.)
Makes a lot!

BEER LENTIL SOUP
A great cruising soup!

2 cups dried lentils
5 12-oz. bottles of beer
1 cup of water
1 ham hock or ham bone
2 medium onions, diced
2 stalks celery, diced
3 medium carrots, sliced
1/4 tsp. pepper
2 tsp. salt

Cook the lentils in the beer and water for one hour. Add other
ingredients and cook another two hours. Remove the ham hock or bone,
cut off any meat, and return the meat to the soup. Serve. Makes 8
cups.

When making split-pea soup, add a slice of bread when you start cooking
the liquid and peas together. This will keep the peas from going to the
bottom and burning or sticking.

To prevent curdling of the milk or cream in tomato soup, add the tomato
soup to the milk rather than vice versa.

BROWN RICE AND CARROT SOUP

1/2 cup long-grain brown rice
2 cups broth
1/4 tsp. marjoram
1/4 tsp. dill seed
3 cups stock
1 1/2 cups diced carrots
1/4 cup chopped parsley
1/8 tsp. pepper
Juice from half a lemon

Cook the rice 30 minutes in the two cups of broth. Add everything else except the lemon juice, and simmer for 45 minutes – 1 hour, or until the carrots are very tender and the rice is nicely puffed. If it hasn't thickened a little by then, add a little flour. Add lemon juice, stir, and serve. Makes 4 cups.

TURKEY SOUP

1 can cream of mushroom soup
1 can cream of chicken soup
2 cans milk
3/4 cup diced turkey

Mix all together and cook on medium-high heat until heated through. Top with fresh parsley. Serves 4.

Photo albums that have sticky, plastic-covered pages are great for keeping recipes that you have cut out of newspapers or magazines, but haven't tried yet. Once you give them a try and decide you like them, you can transfer them to a more permanent home.

Soups, Chowders, & Chilies

TORTILLA SOUP

1/2 cup onions, chopped
4 oz. green chilies, chopped
4 cups chicken broth
2 cups long-grain white rice, cooked
10 oz. tomatoes and green chilies, undrained
5 oz. chicken breast strips, cooked and cubed
1 Tbsp. lime juice
Tortilla chips

In a large saucepan, cook onions and chilies until tender. Add broth, rice, tomatoes, and chicken cubes. Mix well. Bring to a boil. Reduce heat. Cover and simmer for 20 minutes. Stir in lime juice. Top each serving with tortilla chips.

Herbs such as bay leaves and garlic cloves do not dissolve as they cook. Skewer them with a toothpick to make them easy to spot and remove.

An easy way to skim the fat from soup or gravy is to make the food a day ahead and refrigerate it. The fat will rise to the top as it cools, and you can remove it easily with a spoon or spatula. If you would rather eat the soup on the day it's made, cool it quickly in the freezer.

Another way to take the grease off soup or gravy is to swish a lettuce leaf gently and slowly over the surface. The lettuce will absorb the grease.

FRESH ONION SOUP WITH SPINACH

One of the best onion soups you will ever taste! It is especially complimented by a crusty garlic/dill loaf, fresh fruit salad, and aged dry red wine. Serves 6-8.

2 Tbsp. olive oil
3 Tbsp. butter
4 cups thinly sliced onions
1 large garlic clove, mashed
1 tsp. salt
1 tsp. pepper
1 1/2 Tbsp. flour
1 cup dry red wine
8 cups beef, chicken, or vegetable broth
10 oz. pre-washed fresh spinach, chopped
2 Tbsp. pastina
6-8 slices of toasted Italian bread
1 1/2 cups grated Parmesan cheese

Combine olive oil and butter in a heavy saucepan and heat. Add onions. Cover and sauté slowly for 12-15 minutes. Uncover and cook slowly to a dark brown. Add garlic, salt, and pepper. Sprinkle in flour and stir. Add wine and simmer for 3 minutes. Add broth, spinach, and pastina; cook for 6-10 minutes or until spinach is cooked.

Pour soup into a crock or individual heat-proof bowls and cover with slices of toast. Cover the entire surface with Parmesan cheese. Place in the broiler under low heat and brown. Serve with extra grated cheese, if desired.

If cutting onions makes you cry, wear swimmers' goggles or a scuba mask. Or chill the onions for at least an hour in the refrigerator beforehand. Or breathe through your mouth while you're cutting.

FRESH MUSHROOM SOUP

When served with a tossed green salad and hot French bread, this recipe will serve 4 discriminating gourmets.

6 Tbsp. butter
1 cup water
1/2 tsp. sugar
1 cup dry vermouth
1/4 cup flour
1/4 tsp. pepper
2 cups onions, minced
1 3/4 cups chicken broth
1 lb. fresh Portobello mushrooms (white mushrooms, while less flavorful, can be substituted)

In a large saucepan, melt butter and cook onions and sugar slowly for about 30-45 minutes or until onions are golden. Slice 1/3 of the mushrooms and sauté for 5 minutes. Stir in flour until smooth. Cook for 2 minutes, stirring constantly. Pour in water and stir until smooth. Add remaining ingredients and heat to boiling, stirring constantly. Reduce heat and simmer uncovered for 10 minutes.

Use an egg slicer to slice all kinds of soft things including kiwis, pears, mushrooms, and soft cheeses, like mozzarella, quickly and uniformly.

To keep mushrooms from becoming slimy, always refrigerate them in a brown paper bag—never plastic. Paper allows the mushrooms to breathe while holding in the humidity that keeps them fresh.

Use bottled clam juice as a quick substitute for fish broth.

CORN CHOWDER

3 Tbsp. butter or margarine
1 cup diced cooked ham
1 cup chopped Louisiana seasoning (onions, bell pepper, shallots)
2 cups chicken broth
1 cup diced potatoes
1 1/2 cups milk
1/2 cup heavy cream
1 17-oz. can whole kernel corn
1 2-oz. jar sliced pimientos, drained

Melt butter in saucepan. Sauté ham and set aside. Sauté seasoning.
Add chicken broth and potatoes. Cover and cook over medium heat
about 20 minutes. Add milk, cream, corn, pimientos, and ham. Reduce
heat and cook until thoroughly heated. Do not boil. Makes 6 servings.

LUNACY CHOWDER

1/2 cup chopped onion
1/2 cup chopped green pepper
2 cups potatoes, cubed
2 Tbsp. cooking oil
2 Tbsp. butter or margarine
1/2 – 1 cup cooking sherry, to taste
1 tsp. minced garlic (from the jar), or 2-3 cloves fresh
1 11-oz. can kernel corn (or creamed)
2 Tbsp. flour (or Bisquick)
1 can chicken broth
1 cup water
1-2 cups milk
1/8 tsp. celery seed
1/2 tsp. dried cilantro (or coriander)

Dash of salt (you won't need much)
Cracked black pepper - lots!
1-2 cups leftover fish, lobster, conch, or shellfish—deboned, deshelled, and cut into cubes. Use whatever is available. Actually, this is pretty good without meat at all!

In large Dutch oven or wok, melt margarine and oil together. Add fresh garlic or garlic salt later. Add onions and peppers and sauté until onions are transparent. Stir in the cubed potatoes and mix to coat them with the oil-margarine mixture. Cook for 2-3 minutes. Stir again and dust the vegetables with flour. Stir to coat and allow to brown slightly. Add the sherry and simmer for 5-10 minutes. Grind in some pepper and a pinch of salt.

Now add the corn (no need to drain.) If there is a lot of liquid, adjust the amounts of water, broth, or milk that you add later. Sprinkle with celery seeds and cilantro or add the fresh herbs. Add more black pepper, especially if you like it spicy. Simmer on medium heat for about half an hour until all vegetables are tender (but retain their identities) and the broth has thickened.

About 20 minutes before serving, add the fish and milk and stir thoroughly. Simmer until flavors have blended and stock has reduced. Garnish with more cracked pepper and fresh parsley, if you have it. Serve thick and bubbly with crusty fresh bread. 4-6 servings.

Left over fish? Make a chilled fresh fish salad using broiled or baked fish left over from last night's dinner. Follow the directions for your favorite tuna fish salad, substituting the cooked and chilled fresh fish. Or, toss the fish with blanched and chilled fresh vegetables and a dressing of oil, lemon or lime juice, and fresh herbs.

Soups, Chowders, & Chilies

EASY CLAM CHOWDER

1 can Healthy Choice Cream of Celery soup
1 can Healthy Choice Cream of Potato soup
1 can baby clams
1 Tbsp. butter or margarine
1 soup can of 1% milk (more or less)
Dash of cayenne pepper

Mix all together and slowly heat over low heat. Stir often.

QUICK CHILI

Shredded cheese
30 oz. chili beans
2 Tbsp. chili powder
3 tsp. ground cumin
1/2 tsp. garlic powder
1 green pepper, chopped
1 lb. lean ground beef
1 medium onion, chopped
6 oz. tomato paste
28 oz. tomato purée

In a large saucepan, brown the beef in the onion over medium-high heat.
Drain off excess fat. Add remaining ingredients and bring to a boil.
Reduce heat and simmer uncovered, over medium-low heat, 10-15
minutes. Top with shredded cheese and serve.

Store spices from the Capsicum genus—paprika, red pepper (cayenne),
and chili powder in dark containers on the refrigerator door
compartments; they deteriorate in heat and high humidity.

BLACK BEAN CHILI

1 1/2 lb. ground beef
2 cloves garlic, minced
Pinch of sugar
1/2 - 1 tsp. cinnamon
1 Tbsp. chili powder
1 15-oz. can black beans and juice
1 28-oz. can diced tomatoes and juice
Parsley flakes

Brown beef. Add spices, beans, and tomatoes. Cook slowly, about 20 minutes. Serve plain, or over pasta or rice. If you prefer the veggie version, eliminate the meat. Resist the temptation to add onion as it detracts from the flavor.

You can grow parsley easily by cutting a small sponge in half and sprinkling a few parsley seeds over the halves. Put the sponges on a dish near a sunny window and make sure to keep them moist.

After opening a box of any pasta product, store unused portion in a tightly covered glass container to preserve freshness.

Use a French-fry basket or a large strainer when cooking pasta. It is so easy to lift the basket out of the water before rinsing the pasta and transferring it to the serving bowl.

Did you know that batteries, film, and hydrogen peroxide stay fresh longer when stored in the refrigerator?

PICNIC SALAD

1 package of frozen English peas
Cauliflower, broken into small pieces
Celery, chopped
Green onion, chopped
Salad dressing

Mix the peas, cauliflower, celery, and onion with salad dressing.
Refrigerate 24 hours before serving. Serve on lettuce and top with lots
of Parmesan cheese. (Note: This will keep well on a long cruise. Mix
everything together, except for salad dressing, and refrigerate. When
ready to serve, add dressing and serve on lettuce with Parmesan cheese.)

BROCCOLI SALAD

Combine:
2 bunches broccoli
12 oz. shredded mozzarella cheese
1 lb. bacon, cooked and crumbled
1/2 small onion

Mix:
1 cup mayonnaise
1/2 cup sugar
2 Tbsp. white vinegar

Combine about 1/2 hour before serving.

Combine all ingredients for an oil-and-vinegar dressing in a screw-top jar.
Add an ice cube and shake. Discard the ice cube and your dressing will
be extra smooth and well mixed.

PEA SALAD

1 package frozen peas, thawed
1/4 cup chopped celery
5 green onions, sliced
2 Tbsp. parsley
Salt and pepper to taste
Mayonnaise and sour cream to coat

Toss everything together; refrigerate for an hour. The perfect salad!

RAMEN NOODLE SALAD

1 large stalk broccoli, cut up
1 head Romaine lettuce, cut up
5 Tbsp. green onion, cut up
3/4 cup margarine
2 packages Ramen noodles, broken up
3/4 cup slivered almonds
1/2 cup sunflower seeds

Mix first 3 ingredients and set aside. Then, sauté noodles (do not use seasoning packet), almonds, and seeds in margarine until brown. Remove from heat and let cool. Add broccoli, lettuce, and onions.

Mix together, shake well, and pour over salad before serving:
1/2 cup salad oil
3 tsp. soy sauce
1/2 cup sugar
1/2 tsp. salt
1/2 cup vinegar

JANE'S CHINESE SALAD

1 head of cabbage, chopped (No time? Buy a bag of pre-chopped slaw)
1 package of chicken-flavored Ramen noodles
1/2 cup toasted sunflower seeds (broil 2 minutes to toast)
2 Tbsp. sesame seeds
3-4 green onions, chopped

Dressing
3 Tbsp. (or less) sugar
3 Tbsp. balsamic vinegar
1/2 cup olive oil
1/4 tsp. pepper
Flavor packet from noodles

Chop cabbage in small pieces and put in a large bowl. Toss in onions, seeds. Break noodles and put on top of the cabbage. Toss with dressing right before serving.

Mix ingredients together at least 1/2 hour before use. Will keep in refrigerator for later use.

For crunch-lovers, top each portion with fat-free pretzels!

To chase insects from cabbage, cauliflower, and similar vegetables, soak the vegetables in cold water with a few tablespoons of either salt or vinegar for fifteen minutes.

To keep insects at bay, place several bay leaves in a cupboard that has been thoroughly scrubbed. This has proven effective against all kinds of pests. The bay leaves last about a year.

MASHED POTATO PATTIES

2 cups mashed potatoes
1 egg white, lightly beaten
2 Tbsp. flour
1/4 cup packaged seasoned breadcrumbs

Mix all ingredients well. Shape into patties 1/2" thick. Cook in a sprayed nonstick skillet 1-2 minutes on each side or until golden brown. Makes 4 servings.

TWICE COOKED POTATOES

Enough potatoes for your crew
1/2 cup olive oil
1/4 cup spike seasoning (Can be purchased at any natural food store. May substitute Mrs. Dash.)
1 Tbsp. garlic powder

Boil potatoes until tender. Cool completely. Quarter potatoes and place in a baking pan. Cover potatoes with oil, spike, and garlic. Bake at 350° until brown and crisp. If you are in a tropical climate and don't want to heat the oven, you can brown in a skillet on top of the stove or on the grill.

Soothe a minor kitchen burn by rubbing it gently with the cut surface of a cold raw potato.

If your raw potatoes become soft, put them in ice water for half an hour and they'll become hard again.

Salads and Vegetables

OYSTER-STUFFED POTATOES

2 large baking potatoes
4 shitake mushrooms, diced
2 cans smoked oysters

Bake potatoes. Drain oysters. Cut baked potatoes in half lengthwise and scoop out potato; mix with oysters and mushrooms. Spoon back into potato skins.

SOUR CREAM SCALLOPED POTATOES
Quick, easy, and delicious!

1 package (2 lbs.) frozen hash brown potatoes
2 cups sour cream
1 can cream of chicken soup
2 cups shredded cheddar cheese
1/2 cup melted butter
1/2 cup chopped onion (or 2 Tbsp. instant)
1 tsp. salt
1/2 tsp. pepper
1 lg. can French-fried onions

Combine all ingredients, except for the French-fried onions, and put into a 2 1/2 quart baking dish. Bake uncovered at 350° for 1 hour. Sprinkle onions over top and bake 10 more minutes.

Lettuce or celery will crisp up quickly if you place it in a pan of cold water, adding a few slices of raw potato.

SAVORY SKILLET POTATOES

1 1/2 pounds all-purpose potatoes, diced
1 large onion, thinly sliced
1 envelope Lipton Recipe Secrets Savory Herb with Garlic soup mix*
2 Tbsp. olive or vegetable oil

In large bowl, toss potatoes, onions, and savory herb with garlic soup mix until potatoes are well-coated.

In a 12-inch nonstick skillet, heat oil over medium-high heat and cook potato mixture, covered, 5 minutes. Remove cover and cook an additional 10 minutes (or until potatoes are tender), stirring frequently. Makes about 6 servings.

* May substitute Lipton Recipe Secrets Onion or Italian Herb with Tomato soup mix.

Place freshly made French-fried potatoes in a paper bag, add salt, and shake. In one easy motion the excess grease is absorbed and the potatoes are salted.

Net shopping bags, also called French shopping bags, are great for storing onions, garlic, and potatoes. They maintain air circulation around these vegetables, which is important for their good keeping.

Store potatoes and whole ginger root together and they will keep each other fresh.

STUFFED ZUCCHINI

3 medium zucchini, unpeeled
1 cup fresh mushrooms, chopped
1 cup Provolone cheese
1 sausage link, skin removed, cut into small pieces
2 Tbsp. flour
1/4 tsp. oregano

Cook zucchini in boiling, salted water for 10 minutes or until tender (don't overcook), then drain and cool. Cut zucchini in half, lengthwise. Scoop out the centers, leaving about a 1/4" shell. Chop the scooped-out zucchini and set aside.

Sauté the skinless sausage until done, then add chopped mushrooms and cook until tender. Stir in flour and oregano. Remove from heat, add cheese, and chopped zucchini.

Fill the zucchini shells with the mixture and sprinkle each with Parmesan cheese. Broil the stuffed zucchini until hot and bubbly. Serve immediately. Serves 6.

EGGPLANT A LA SNOWBIRD

1 large eggplant, cut in 1/2" thick slices
Olive oil
Balsamic vinegar (or red wine vinegar)
1 Tbsp. chopped garlic
Salt and cracked pepper to taste

Pre-heat oven to 350°. Dip sliced eggplant in olive oil. Place eggplant slices on cookie sheet. Sprinkle chopped garlic over eggplant. Bake for

Salads and Vegetables

about 20 minutes until eggplant is soft. Take out of oven and pour 1/3 cup of vinegar over the eggplant and slip under broiler (this step is not crucial, so don't worry if you don't have a broiler.) Put on plate and let it come to room temperature.

You can use zucchini and yellow summer squash the same way.

A good rule of thumb: If eggplant is to be cooked for a short time, peel off the skin. If it is to be cooked longer, peeling isn't necessary.

To get the skins off garlic before chopping, pound each clove with the side of a heavy knife or a bottle. The skin pops right off.

A handy oil dispenser: Put your cooking oil in a clean, well-rinsed dish detergent bottle. You will find that the squirt top makes pouring oil cleaner and easier than having to deal with a screw-on cap.

Keep your shopping list attached to your refrigerator. That way, when someone uses the last bit of a food or grocery item, he or she can note that it needs replenishing.

The next time you make mashed potatoes, try this: Instead of using milk, mix powdered milk with the water that was used to cook the potatoes.

Prevent mildew from forming in your refrigerator by wiping it down with vinegar. The acid effectively kills mildew fungi.

GRILLED VEGETABLE QUESADILLAS

1 ear of corn, shucked and desilked
1 red bell pepper, cut in half, seeds and ribs removed
1 medium yellow squash, ends trimmed, cut in half length-wise
1/2 small onion
Vegetable oil spray
4 oz. shredded, low-fat Monterey Jack cheese (about 1 cup)
1 Italian plum tomato, diced
2 tsp. lime juice
1/4 tsp. chili powder
1/8 tsp. pepper
4 6-inch corn tortillas
1/2 cup salsa
1/2 cup non-fat or low-fat sour cream

Lightly spray all surfaces of corn, bell pepper, squash, and onion with vegetable oil spray.

Over medium-hot coals (or medium-high heat if using gas, electric, propane, or stove-top grill), grill corn on all sides until done, about 2 minutes per side; bell pepper, squash, and onion should take 1-2 minutes. Places vegetables on a cutting board; let cool for about 10 minutes.

Dice bell pepper, squash, and onion and place in a medium bowl. Using a sharp knife, slice corn kernels off cob. Stir corn, cheese, tomato, lime juice, chili powder, and pepper into vegetable mixture. Set aside.

Pre-heat a nonstick griddle or cast-iron skillet over medium heat. Using vegetable oil spray, lightly spray one side of a tortilla. Place tortilla, sprayed side down, on the griddle. Spread a heaping 1/3 cup of the vegetable/cheese mixture on half of the tortilla. Fold the other half of the tortilla over the filling. Cook for 1-2 minutes on each side, or until tortilla is golden-brown and cheese is melted. Remove and place on a cutting board. Repeat with remaining tortillas and filling.

To serve, cut quesadillas in half and place on serving platter. Top each quesadilla with 1 tablespoon each of salsa and sour cream.

CHILI CON QUESO CASSEROLE

2 4-oz. cans mild, whole green chilies, drained
2 cups chopped tomatoes (2-3 medium)
2 cups shredded cheddar cheese (8 oz.)
1 cup Bisquick baking mix
1/2 cup dairy sour cream
1/2 cup milk
3 eggs

Heat oven to 375°. Grease square baking dish, 8" x 8" x 2". Remove seeds from chilies. Arrange chilies in single layer in dish. Sprinkle with tomatoes and cheese. Beat remaining ingredients with wire whisk or hand beater until smooth. Pour over top. Bake uncovered 35-40 minutes. Test by inserting knife in center; should come out clean. Makes 6-8 servings.

Take a tip from those who know in sunny Mexico: Eating chilies and other hot, spicy foods in hot weather will actually cool you off by stimulating your circulation and causing you to perspire.

The oil in chili peppers is so pungent it can actually burn your skin. Washing irritated areas in vinegar water will bring much more relief than just soap and water.

TACO AND BLACK BEAN SKILLET DINNER
Ready in 30 minutes!

1 24-oz. jar Old El Paso Thick 'n Chunky salsa or picante
1 4.6-oz. package Old El Paso taco shells (12 shells)
1 cup shredded Monterey Jack cheese
1 cup shredded cheddar cheese
1 small onion, chopped
1 11-oz. can Green Giant white corn, drained (may use yellow corn)
1 4.5-oz. can Old El Paso chopped green chilies
1 15-oz. can black beans
2 tsp. cumin
1 Tbsp. steak sauce

Spray deep 10" skillet with nonstick cooking spray. Spread 1 cup of salsa over bottom of skillet. Break each taco shell into 4-6 pieces. Arrange half of the broken shells over salsa. Spread 1 cup of the remaining salsa over shells. Sprinkle with 1/2 cup of each of the Monterey Jack and cheddar cheeses. Top with onion, corn, and green chilies.

In small bowl, combine beans, cumin, and steak sauce; mix well. Spoon evenly over mixture in skillet. Top with remaining broken shells, cheeses, and salsa. Cover. Cook over medium-low heat for 15-20 minutes or until mixture is bubbly and cheese is melted.

To serve, top with 1/2 cup sour cream and, if desired, garnish with cilantro, tomatoes, olives, jalapeno chilies and guacamole.

Include in your staples dried soup mixes for dips (onion, vegetable without noodles, cream of leek, etc.) Buy the bases (sour cream, cream cheese, cottage cheese, yogurt, etc.) when needed.

VEGGIE PIZZA

2 cans Pillsbury refrigerated pizza dough
1 8-oz. block of cream cheese, softened
1 cup mayonnaise
1 package Knorr's vegetable soup mix
Vegetables of your choice: sliced cherry tomatoes, carrots, green
pepper, mushrooms, broccoli

Bake pizza crust according to package directions. Cool. Mix cream
cheese with mayo and vegetable soup mix. Spread on crusts. Top with
fresh veggies. Cut into squares.

VEGGIE SUPREME

Here's an easy one! Feel free to experiment, substituting any of your
favorite vegetables or cheeses for those listed here.

2 tomatoes, sliced
2 cups mushrooms, sliced
1/2 cup onion, thinly sliced
1 green pepper, sliced
Salt and pepper to taste
1 cup Mozzarella cheese, shredded
5 oz. pizza sauce
12" Boboli Italian pizza crust

Preheat oven to 450°. Spread sauce on pizza crust leaving a 1" border.
Pile on the veggies. Be creative! Sprinkle with cheese. Bake 8-10
minutes on baking sheet in lower third of oven. Serve immediately.

Pizza, bacon, and chicken cuts more easily with scissors.

PIZZA ON THE BEACH

Dough
1 package dry yeast
1 tsp. sugar
1 cup warm water
2 cups white flour
1 cup whole wheat flour
1/4 tsp. salt
1 tsp. olive oil (plus extra oil to brush on dough)
If desired: garlic powder, basil, oregano

Dissolve yeast and sugar in water. Let stand 5-10 minutes. Mix flour and salt in a large bowl. Stir to make dough soft. Turn onto floured surface. Knead 5-10 minutes. Divide into 6 pieces. Roll out each piece and put on paper plates. Coat one side with olive oil. Place in skillet on slow fire until brown on one side.

Coat other side with oil and turn browned side up. Top with sauce, cheese, and toppings. Return to grill. Cook until cheese is melted.

Another option is to divide the dough in half, rather than 6 pieces. Roll out each half and fit onto a rectangular cookie sheet. Cook the crust about 7-10 minutes in a 400° oven, turn over, spread with sauce, cheese, and toppings. Return to oven and bake until cheese is melted.

Try hard-wheat or pasta flour (available at health food stores) for a beautiful golden-brown pizza crust.

No need to buy a special baking tile to produce a crisp bottom on your pizza and French bread. An unglazed terra-cotta tile purchased from a flooring or tile store works just as well.

PASTA POWER

This one-dish pasta meal is packed with carbohydrates and fiber and is low in fat.

1/2 – 3/4 lb. spaghetti (vermicelli)
3 Tbsp. fresh chopped basil
2 tsp. olive oil or cooking spray
3 Tbsp. fresh chopped parsley
1 medium onion, chopped
Dash of fresh ground pepper
20 snow pea pods
1/2 – 3/4 cup plain, nonfat yogurt
2 stalks fresh broccoli, chopped
1/4 cup (1 oz.) grated Parmesan cheese
1 zucchini, sliced
1/2 cup kidney beans, cooked or canned, drained
5 mushrooms, chopped

Cook pasta according to directions; drain. Heat oil in large skillet (or spray with vegetable oil cooking spray) and cook onion until glossy. Add pea pods, mushrooms, broccoli, zucchini, and kidney beans. Stir in basil, parsley, and pepper. Sauté vegetables until tender but still crunchy. Add sautéed veggies to pasta. Toss with yogurt and cheese. Serve immediately. Makes 4 servings.

Three ways to prevent boilovers:
1. Lay a large spoon or spatula across the top of the pot to reduce boilovers and splashing water while cooking.
2. Coat the top of the pot with shortening.
3. Add a few drops of cooking oil or a pat of margarine to the water. This also presents the pasta from sticking together.

E-Z PASTA SALAD

1 1-lb. Box bow-tie pasta, cooked to desired doneness
1 green bell pepper, cut in thin strips
1 red bell pepper, cut in thin strips
1 small can sliced black olives, drained
1 cucumber, sliced
Cherry tomatoes, halved
Italian salad dressing
Salt and pepper to taste

Mix all ingredients in large bowl, using enough salad dressing to coat the ingredients.

PEPPY PARMESAN PASTA
Ready in 20 minutes. Serves 4.

8 oz. angel hair pasta
1 large tomato, chopped
1 3-oz. package sliced pepperoni
1 small can ripe olives, drained (approx. 2 ounces)
1/4 cup grated Parmesan cheese
3 Tbsp. olive or vegetable oil
1/2 tsp. salt or salt-free seasoning blend
1/4 tsp. garlic powder

Cook pasta according to package directions. Meanwhile, combine the tomato, pepperoni, olives, Parmesan cheese, oil, salt (if desired) and garlic powder in a serving bowl. Drain pasta; add to tomato mixture. Toss to coat.

To keep cheese from hardening, butter the cut end.

GINI'S SPAGHETTI SALAD

1 can broccoli cheese soup
1 Tbsp. butter
1 1/2 cups cooked chicken, cut into strips
3 cups cooked fettuccine
1 clove garlic, minced
1 cup milk
1/4 cup Parmesan cheese, grated
Fresh parsley, to taste

Cook garlic in the butter in a large skillet over medium-high heat. Add soup, milk, and Parmesan cheese. Bring to a boil and reduce heat. Add chicken and simmer for 5 minutes, stirring often. Toss the fettuccine with the chicken mixture. Sprinkle with fresh parsley.

CHICKEN & ASPARAGUS PASTA

1 lb. asparagus, cut into 2" pieces
1 cup Balsamic vinegar dressing
1 cup grilled chicken breast strips
2 cups pasta bow ties, cooked
8 oz. Portobello mushrooms
2 Tbsp. sun-dried tomatoes

Cook mushrooms and asparagus in a large skillet with 1/4 cup balsamic vinegar dressing. Stir frequently, cooking until tender. Add remaining balsamic vinegar dressing and the tomatoes, pasta, and chicken strips. Cover and cook over medium heat until heated through.

To prevent mold, store cheese in a tightly covered container with a few sugar cubes.

EASY RIGATONI

1 1/2 lb. Italian sausage
2 large green peppers
1 large onion, chopped
2 cans (7 1/2-oz. each) Hunts Spaghetti Sauce
10 oz. uncooked rigatoni pasta

Brown sausage in 5 qt. Dutch oven. Add peppers and onion. Cook until tender. Stir in spaghetti sauce. Stir in uncooked pasta. Cover and bake 30 minutes in 375° oven until pasta is tender. Serves 8-10.

LAZY DAY LASAGNE

6 oz. lasagne noodles, cooked according to package directions
1/4 tsp. dried oregano, crushed
1 15.5-oz can spaghetti sauce
1 cup cream-style cottage cheese
1 6-oz. packaged sliced mozzarella cheese

Combine oregano and spaghetti sauce. In a greased 10" x 6" x 1 1/2" baking dish, make layers: half each noodles, cottage cheese, mozzarella cheese slices, and spaghetti sauce. Repeat. Bake at 375° for 30 minutes. Allow to cool 10 minutes before serving. Serves 4.

Use a potato peeler to cut cheese into strips for salads and other garnishings.

Warm the knife before cutting cheese; the cheese will cut as easily as butter.

PASTA WITH TOMATO AND BASIL

1 package fresh angel hair pasta
6 plum tomatoes
6 fresh basil leaves
1 bunch green onions
4 cloves garlic
1 rib celery
10 seedless green olives, halved
1 Tbsp. crushed red pepper
1/2 cup white wine
Olive oil
Fresh Parmesan cheese, grated

Heat water to cook pasta. Meanwhile, quarter tomatoes, set aside. Chop onions, garlic, and celery; set aside. Cook pasta according to package directions. Add 1 Tbsp. of olive oil to a heavy skillet (more if necessary.) Heat oil. Add onions, garlic, and celery and sauté one minute. Add additional oil and tomatoes; toss gently until tomatoes are soft. Add chopped basil leaves and stir gently for one minute. Add crushed red peppers; mix. Add wine. Add cooked pasta to vegetables and toss gently. Add sliced olives. Serve into pasta bowls and top with parmesan cheese. Serve with hot fresh French bread. Serves 4.

HOT TAMALE SHELLS

1 package Velveeta Shells and Cheese Dinner
1 4-oz. can chopped green chilies
1 2 1/4-oz. can pitted ripe olive slices
Salsa

Prepare dinner as directed on package. Stir in green chilies and ripe olive slices. Add salsa, if desired, at table.

Meatless Meals and Pasta

PASTA PARMESAN

Mix and simmer for 10 minutes:
2 cloves garlic, minced
1 red onion, minced
2 cups fat-free chicken stock

Add:
1 cup Parmesan cheese
1 cup nonfat sour cream
1/4 cup fresh parsley, chopped

Toss with cooked pasta.

PASTA WITH GARLIC CLAM SAUCE

1 tsp. chopped garlic (from a jar)
1 14 oz. can diced tomatoes
1 6 oz. can minced clams, undrained
1 tsp. sugar
3 Tbsp. chopped fresh parsley
6 oz. pasta, cooked

Mix everything except the pasta in a medium pan. Bring to a boil over medium heat. Lower heat and simmer for 10 minutes. Serve over cooked pasta. Makes 3 servings.

Cottage cheese stays fresher longer if stored upside down in the refrigerator.

Chicken

CHICKEN STROGANOFF

1 8-oz. package noodles
1 package onion soup mix
4 Tbsp. sour cream (made from dry mix)
1 6-oz. can chicken
1 small can sliced mushrooms

Following directions for soup, bring water to a boil; add onion soup. Mix and stir until dissolved. Add noodles with the soup and cook until tender, 8-10 minutes. Drain water carefully, keeping as much of the onion as possible. Add sour cream, mushrooms, and chicken. Season to taste.

CHICKEN VERA CRUZ

2 1/2 – 3 lb. chicken, cut up
2 Tbsp. oil
1 lb. can whole tomatoes
1 1/2 cup water
1 cup uncooked long grain rice
1 package Sloppy Joe mix
1 package chicken gravy mix
1 package frozen peas

Brown chicken in olive oil with some salt and pepper. Add tomatoes, water, rice, and mixes. Stir well to mix ingredients and loosen particles from the bottom of the pot. Cook uncovered for 20 minutes. Add peas and cook until rice is done and peas are tender, about 15 minutes. Serves 4.

Did you know that plastic wrap will be easier to manage if kept stored in the refrigerator?

QUICK CHICKEN TETRAZZINI
An Italian salad makes a terrific accompaniment.

4 cups water
16 oz. chicken broth
1 tsp. salt
1/4 tsp. pepper
8 oz. egg noodles
2 cups cooked chicken, cubed
1 4-oz. can mushrooms, drained
1/4 cup pimiento, chopped
1/4 cup flour
1 cup milk
Parmesan cheese

In a large pot, bring water, broth, salt, and pepper to a boil. Add
noodles. Bring back to a boil. Reduce heat and cook for 5 minutes,
stirring occasionally. Blend flour with milk and add chicken, mushrooms,
and pimiento. Simmer, stirring constantly, until mixture thickens, about
5 minutes. Serve in bowls and sprinkle with Parmesan cheese. Serves 4.

COCONUT MILK CHICKEN

1 medium chicken, cut into serving pieces
1 can coconut milk
1 medium-large onion, chopped
4-6 cloves garlic, crushed
3 Tbsp. vinegar
3 Tbsp. cooking oil
1 cup water, sprinkled with paprika

Heat oil and sauté garlic until golden brown. Reduce heat and add onion,
cooking until transparent.

68

Add chicken and sauté until brown. Add water and vinegar at the same time. DO NOT STIR UNTIL IT COMES TO A BOIL. Boil for 5-8 minutes. Add salt to taste and a little water. Cover the pan and cook until chicken is tender. Add coconut milk and simmer for about 3 minutes. Serve over rice. Makes 4 servings.

GARLICY CHICKEN BREASTS

6 boneless, skinless chicken breasts
1/2 cup grated Parmesan cheese
1 package Good Seasonings roasted garlic or Italian dressing mix

In a medium bowl, stir together dressing mix and Parmesan cheese. Moisten each chicken breast in water and dip into the dressing mixture and place in a shallow baking dish. Bake at 400° for 20-25 minutes or until cooked through.

CHICKEN QUESADILLAS

4-5 small flour or corn tortillas
1 small onion
1 6-oz. can chicken
1 tsp. oil
4 oz. Monterey Jack cheese (with jalapeño peppers, if you like it spicy)

Dice onion. Slice cheese in thin slices. Drain the chicken. Assemble quesadillas by sprinkling chicken, onion, and cheese on half of the tortilla. Fold the tortilla over omelet-style and lightly brown in oil.

Avoid buying chicken on Monday. It is likely you will get one that wasn't bought by the weekend.

69

Chicken

BAKED CHICKEN BREASTS

4-6 chicken breasts
1 stick butter (or margarine)
1 envelope Good Seasons Italian dressing mix
2 Tbsp. prepared mustard (French's)

Pre-heat oven to 350°. Mix butter, salad dressing mix, and mustard. Lay chicken in baking pan or dish. Spoon butter mix over chicken. Bake uncovered 45 minutes or until done, basting once.

If using less butter, cut back on seasonings. The basting butter is delicious spooned over rice, noodles, or potatoes. Leftover chicken is great for salads or sandwiches.

LOW-FAT CHICKEN ENCHILADAS

12 corn tortillas
2 cups grated reduced-fat Monterey Jack cheese
3/4 cup chopped onion
1/4 cup butter (Butter Buds is fine)
3 Tbsp. flour
2 cups fat-free chicken broth
1 cup fat-free sour cream
2 cups diced boned chicken
1 cup chopped green chilies

Melt butter in large skillet and blend in flour. Add broth slowly to prevent lumps and cook until thick. Stir in sour cream, chicken, and peppers.

Soften tortillas in a moistened paper towel. Put 4-5 tortillas between moistened paper towels and microwave on high 4-5 minutes.

70

Place 2 Tbsp. of the cheese and 1 Tbsp. of the onion in each tortilla and roll up. Place seam-side down in casserole dish. Pour chicken sauce over tortilla; sprinkle with remaining cheese. Bake at 350° for 30 minutes.

MEXICAN CHICKEN & RICE DINNER
Ready in 15 minutes. Yields 4 servings.

1 Tbsp. oil
4 small boneless skinless chicken breast halves (about 1 lb.)
2 cups water
1 cup thick 'n chunky salsa
2 cups Minute Rice, uncooked
1 8-oz. can whole kernel corn, drained
1 cup shredded cheddar cheese

Heat oil in large nonstick skillet on medium-high heat. Add chicken; cover. Cook 4 minutes on each side or until cooked through. Remove chicken from skillet. Stir in water and salsa; bring to boil. Stir in rice and corn. Top with chicken. Sprinkle chicken with cheese; cover. Cook on low heat 5 minutes. Stir and serve.

Defrost a frozen chicken by soaking it in cold water that has been heavily salted. This draws out blood, and the breast meat will be pure white.

To keep fresh chicken fresher, immediately remove polyethylene wrap, loosely wrap chicken in waxed paper, and refrigerate. Fresh chicken should be used within three days.

Chicken

SAN ANTONIO CHICKEN SKILLET

2 large onions, coarsely chopped
2 cloves garlic
1/4 cup vegetable oil
10 oz. vermicelli, broken into pieces
2 cups cooked chicken (or turkey), diced
1 16-oz. can whole tomatoes
1 14-oz. can chicken broth
3/4 cup picanté sauce
1 tsp. ground cumin
1 large green pepper, cut in short, thin strips
1/2 cup cheddar cheese, shredded
1/4 cup cilantro, chopped (optional)

Cook onion and garlic in oil in 12" skillet over medium heat for 2 minutes.
Stir in chicken, tomatoes, broth, picanté sauce, and cumin. Simmer,
stirring occasionally and breaking up tomatoes with spoon, 3 minutes.
Add green pepper. Continue to simmer until pasta is tender and most of
liquid is absorbed, 4-5 minutes. Sprinkle with cheese and, if desired,
cilantro. Serve with additional picanté sauce.

COUSCOUS WITH CHICKEN IN TARRAGON CREAM SAUCE

2 tsp. olive oil
4 boneless skinless chicken breasts, cut into strips
3 cups sliced fresh mushrooms
1 jar chicken gravy
1 tsp. dried tarragon leaves, crushed
1 1/4 cups chicken broth
1 cup frozen baby sweet peas
1 cup uncooked couscous

72

Chicken

Spray large nonstick skillet with nonstick cooking spray. Add oil; heat over medium-high heat until hot.

Add chicken, cook and stir 4 minutes. Add mushrooms; cook and stir 4-5 minutes more until tender.

Stir in gravy and tarragon. Reduce heat to medium; cover and cook 5 minutes until thoroughly heated.

In medium saucepan, bring broth and peas to a boil. Remove from heat; stir in couscous. Cover. Let stand 5-6 minutes or until all liquid is absorbed.

To serve, spray small (6 oz.) bowl with nonstick cooking spray. Tightly pack 3/4 cup couscous mixture into bowl. Invert onto center of warm dinner plate; remove bowl, spoon a small amount of sauce over couscous. Spoon chicken mixture around base of couscous. Repeat for 3 remaining servings.

Use kitchen scissors to debone chicken. It's easier and safer than using a knife.

Removing the skin from chicken parts before or after cooking doesn't affect the fat content. But eating it does! About two thirds of the fat is in the skin.

Never leave cooked or raw chicken at room temperature for more than one hour. Refrigerate it promptly because bacteria that can make you sick grow quickly at room temperatures!

QUICK CHICKEN CASSEROLE

2 large potatoes
2 sliced onions
3 pounds cooked chicken
1 can leek and potato soup OR cream of mushroom soup
1/2 cup chicken stock
1 can water
1 cup frozen peas or mixed vegetables
Lemon juice
1/2 cup breadcrumbs
1/3 cup grated cheese

Slice the potatoes and layer at the bottom of dish. Add onions. Cover with soup. Add chicken stock mixed with a can of water. Microwave on high for 10 minutes.

Add cooked chicken and vegetables to dish. Season with black pepper and a squeeze of lemon juice. Mix well. Top with breadcrumbs and grated cheese. Bake at 325° for 15-20 minutes.

CHICKEN PILAF

1/4 cup butter or margarine
1 1/3 cups Minute Rice
1 4-oz. can sliced mushrooms, drained (reserve liquid)
1 Tbsp. minced onion
2 small cans boned chicken
2 Tbsp. raisins
2 tsp. curry powder
1/4 tsp. ground ginger
1 tsp. salt

Chicken

Melt butter in saucepan or skillet. Add rice. Cook until light brown over medium heat, stirring constantly. Remove from heat. Combine mushroom liquid with enough water to measure 1 1/2 cups. Add to saucepan with mushrooms and all remaining ingredients. Stir with fork. Bring to boil. Cover. Remove from heat and let stand 5 minutes. Serves 4.

SAVORY CRESCENT CHICKEN SQUARES

3 oz. softened cream cheese
3 Tbsp. melted butter
2 cups cooked, chopped chicken or turkey (may use canned)
1/4 tsp. salt
1/8 tsp. pepper
2 Tbsp. milk
1 Tbsp. chopped onion
8-oz. can Pillsbury Crescent Rolls
3/4 cup seasoned croutons, crushed (may use less, if desired)

Preheat oven to 350°. Blend cream cheese and 2 Tbsp. of the butter until smooth. Add next 6 ingredients; mix well. Separate crescent dough into 4 rectangles; firmly press perforations to seal. Spoon 1/2 cup of mixture into center of each rectangle. Pull 4 corners of dough to top center; twist slightly and seal edges. Brush with remaining butter and sprinkle with crumbs. Bake on ungreased cookie sheet 20-25 minutes or until golden brown.

When finished preparing chicken, clean all working surfaces with a solution of one part bleach to four parts water. Leave solution on surfaces for 5 seconds before rinsing well with cold water.

Chicken

JIM'S FAVORITE HOMEMADE CHICKEN POT PIE

Mix and pour into bottom of unbaked double pie crust:

1 can cream of chicken soup*
2 cups cooked chicken (leftover turkey works well, too)
1/2 cup sour cream*
1 can mixed vegetables, drained well
Chopped onion to taste
Pepper to taste

Affix top crust and make slits to allow for steam to escape. Bake at 400° 10-15 minutes. Reduce heat to 375° and bake 25-30 more minutes, until browned. Allow to cool slightly before cutting.

*Reduced fat soup and fat-free sour cream may be used, but some of the taste is lost and it takes longer to set up.

LEMONADE CHICKEN

1 6-oz. carton frozen lemonade, thawed
1/3 cup white wine Worcestershire sauce
1 tsp. soy sauce
4 chicken breast halves, skin removed

Mix first three ingredients and pour over chicken. Marinate for an hour. Place chicken in 9" square pan. Bake uncovered at 350° for 1 hour, basting occasionally. Makes 4 servings.

When freezing chicken, wrap parts separately in foil or freezer wrap. This makes it easy to defrost only the amount you need. Proper wrapping prevents "freezer burn," which results from contact with air.

Chicken

CHICKEN TERIYAKI

4 chicken breasts
McCormick's Grill Mates chicken seasoning
1 cup teriyaki sauce

Place chicken breasts in a shallow dish and cover with your favorite
Teriyaki sauce. Sprinkle surface with Grill Mates seasoning. Turn
breasts over to coat well with sauce and seasoning. Allow to marinate in
the refrigerator for at least 30 minutes.

Pre-heat grill or broiler. Cook chicken approximately 6-8 minutes per
side, turning once.

Serve over a bed of salad greens with ranch dressing.

SPICY CHICKEN

4 boneless, skinless chicken breast halves
1 onion, sliced
1 bell pepper, sliced
1 tsp. chopped garlic (from a jar)
1 10-oz. can diced tomatoes and green chilies
2 tsp. paprika

Pound chicken until each piece is very thin and has doubled in size. Cook
in a large, sprayed, nonstick skillet 2 minutes on each side. Remove and
place in a baking dish. Sauté onion and pepper, stirring constantly for 2
minutes. Add garlic and continue to cook 1 more minute. Add tomatoes
and paprika. Bring to a boil and simmer 1 minute. Pour over chicken.
Cover and bake 30 minutes at 350°.

ALICE'S RESTAURANT CHINESE CHICKEN

4 lbs. chicken, cut up

Marinade
1 cup soy sauce
1 cup dry sherry
1 large garlic clove, minced
1 tsp. fresh ginger root, minced

Sauce
1/2 cup Hoisin sauce
1 cup dry sherry
1/2 cup ketchup
1/4 cup brown sugar, packed
1 garlic clove, minced

Combine marinade ingredients and pour over chicken pieces in a shallow pan. Marinate overnight, turning pieces occasionally if all the pieces are not submerged in the marinade. Combine sauce ingredients and set aside. Remove chicken from marinade and drain. Place chicken in a shallow baking pan and cover with the sauce. Bake at 350° for 45 minutes or until done, turning only once. Baste several times while baking. Makes 4 servings.

CHICKEN MARSALA

6 boneless, skinless chicken breast halves
1 tsp. chopped garlic from a jar
8 fresh mushrooms, sliced
1/2 cup Marsala wine

Chicken

Pound chicken until each piece is very thin and has doubled in size. Sauté the garlic and mushrooms in a large, sprayed, nonstick skillet over medium heat for 2-3 minutes. Remove mushrooms.

Cook chicken 2-3 minutes on each side. Remove the chicken and keep warm. Add mushrooms and wine to the pan and heat for 1 minute. Place chicken on a serving plate and pour mushrooms and pan juices over.

CHICKEN AND VEGGIE BAKE

1 can cream of chicken soup
1/2 cup milk
3 cups cooked vegetables (i.e. broccoli, carrots, green beans)
2 5-oz. cans chicken, drained
Dash of Worcestershire sauce
1 can Durkee's French fried onions

Mix soup, milk, vegetables, chicken, Worcestershire, and 1/2 can onions in a 1 1/2 quart casserole. Bake at 350° for 25 minutes or until hot. Stir. Add remaining onions and stir again. Bake 5 minutes longer. Serves 4.

Product dating is not required by Federal regulations, but many stores and processors voluntarily date packages of chicken or chicken products. If a calendar date is shown, immediately adjacent to the date there must be a phrase explaining the meaning of that date such as sell by or use before.

The use-by date is for quality assurance; after the date, peak quality begins to lessen but the product may still be used. It's always best to buy a product before the date expires. If a use-by date expires while the chicken is frozen, the food can still be used.

Chicken

GREEK CHICKEN
For lemon and lime lovers.

4 chicken breasts
2 large potatoes, sliced
Olive oil (equal parts mixed with lemon or lime juice)
Cavender's Greek seasoning, to taste
Salt and pepper, to taste

Marinate chicken breasts in Ziploc bag with all ingredients except
potatoes for several hours. Marinate potatoes in separate bag.
Marinade should be enough to coat chicken and potatoes without excess
use of oil. Put together in pan, potatoes on bottom, and bake at 350°
until done.

GRILLED CHICKEN BREASTS

4 boneless, skinless chicken breasts
1/2 cup soy sauce
1/2 cup Worcestershire sauce
1/2 cup white wine
1 tsp. garlic powder
1 tsp. dried oregano
1 tsp. dried thyme
1 tsp. crushed red pepper

Mix all ingredients and mix with wire whisk. Pour over chicken, cover
with plastic wrap, and marinate in refrigerator overnight. Cook on grill,
medium heat, 10 minutes on each side.

Use small baskets to keep condiments, cheeses, and other small products
from shifting in the refrigerator.

80

Chicken

EASY CHICKEN PAPRIKA

1 Tbsp. vegetable oil
6 boneless, skinless chicken breasts
1 large onion, sliced
1 1/2 cups milk
2 Tbsp. paprika
1 can cream of chicken soup
1 bell pepper, cut into strips
4 cups hot cooked egg noodles

Heat oil in large skillet over medium heat until hot. Cook chicken and onion in oil, turning chicken until it is brown and onion until tender. Drain. Mix milk, paprika, and soup; pour over chicken and onion. Stir in bell pepper. Heat to boiling, stirring occasionally. Reduce heat.

Cover and simmer about 15 minutes longer, or until juice of chicken is no longer pink when centers of thickest pieces are cut. Serve over noodles.

The chicken is a descendant of the Southeast Asian red jungle fowl first domesticated in India around 2000 B.C. Most of the birds raised for meat in America today are from the Cornish (a British breed) and the White Rock (a breed developed in New England). Broiler-fryers, roasters, stewing/baking hens, capons and Rock Cornish hens are all chickens.

Did you know? Inspection is mandatory but grading is voluntary. Chickens are graded according to USDA Agricultural Marketing Service regulations and standards for meatiness, appearance and freedom from defects. Grade A chickens have plump, meaty bodies and clean skin, free of bruises, broken bones, feathers, cuts and discoloration.

OPEN FACE CHICKEN CORDON BLUE
A good dish for company.

4 boneless, skinless chicken breasts
1 Tbsp. margarine
1/2 tsp. pepper
4 slices ham, regular size sandwich slices (not deli-thin)
4 slices Swiss cheese

Preheat oven to 375°. Pound chicken breasts to flatten. Melt margarine in nonstick skillet over medium heat. Cook chicken 1 minute on each side. Sprinkle each side with pepper. Place in a 9" square pan.

Top each chicken breast with a slice of ham. Pour pan drippings over chicken. Cover with foil and bake in preheated oven for 25 minutes. Uncover and add a slice of cheese to the top of each chicken breast. Cover and return to oven for 5 more minutes.

For cleaner broiling, put a thin layer of water in the broiling pan before broiling meat, fish, or poultry. This makes the pan easier to clean later, and the fat doesn't smoke as much.

If you run out of twine to truss your chicken or turkey, use waxed dental floss. It doesn't burn, and you can tie knots in it without it tearing. Not to mention it's cheaper than trussing string.

We continue getting positive comments about canned meats from Brinkman Turkey Farms. Contact them at 16314 US Rt. 68, Findlay, OH 45840, Phone 419-365-5127, Fax 419-365-1284, http://www.brinkmanfarms.com/

Beef

SYMPHONY CASSEROLE

1 1/2 lb. lean ground beef
2 packages Lawry's spaghetti sauce mix
15-oz. can tomato sauce
1 cup water
1 8-oz. package cooked noodles
2 Tbsp. margarine
1 cup sour cream
1 cup low-fat cottage cheese
1 8-oz. package cream cheese
6 oz. shredded sharp cheddar cheese

Brown ground beef and drain off fat. Add spaghetti sauce mix, tomato sauce, and water; simmer 20 minutes. Prepare noodles according to package directions; after draining, return to pot. Add margarine and toss gently until melted. Mix sour cream, cottage cheese, and cream cheese until blended. Stir into noodles.

In large greased casserole dish, layer 1/2 noodle mixture, 1/2 spaghetti sauce, then layer remaining noodles and sauce. Top with shredded cheese. Cover and refrigerate at least 6 hours.

Bake uncovered at 350° for 30-35 minutes. Serves 8-10.

Vacuum packing is a wonderful method of keeping meat fresh longer. If you don't have a home vacuum packer, ask the butcher or supermarket to package it for you. Many do this at no charge. One Sea Sister reported that during a passage with refrigeration, but no freezer, vacuum packed meat (beef, pork & chicken) was still fresh at the end of 3 weeks.

GROUND BEEF NOODLE CASSEROLE

Mix:
2-3 oz. softened cream cheese
1/2 cup evaporated milk
2 tsp. lemon juice
1/4 tsp. garlic salt
1 tsp. Worcestershire sauce

Toss with 5 cups cooked noodles and pour into lightly greased casserole dish.

Cook until tender:
1/2 cup onion
1/4 cup green pepper
1 Tbsp. butter

Add:
1 lb. lean ground beef and brown.

Stir in 8 oz. can tomato sauce and 1/2 cup ketchup. Cook over medium heat 8 minutes until it thickens. Spread over noodles. Bake at 375° for 10 minutes.

"Whatever the meal, I plan ahead. If meals require chopped onions, green peppers, shredded cheese or lettuce, etc., I do all the chopping and shredding at home and place in Ziploc bags. I do the same with meals that require ground beef mixtures or diced chicken/pork. I cook the meat mixtures ahead of time and place in Ziploc bags. On board, all that's left to do is add remaining ingredients, assemble, and cook or heat."

Beef

BEEF STROGANOFF WITH NOODLES

3/4 lbs. wide egg noodles
2 lb. boneless sirloin, cut into 2 1/2" x 1/4" strips
1/2 cup flour (more if needed)
1 tsp. salt
1/4 tsp. pepper
1/3 cup oil
1 large onion, sliced
3/4 lb. fresh mushrooms, cleaned and sliced
1 1/2 cup beef broth
1/2 tsp. crushed sweet basil
1/2 tsp. paprika
1 1/2 cup sour cream

Cook noodles according to directions to desired doneness. Drain and crisp in cold water. Coat meat strips with a mixture of flour, salt, and pepper. Brown meat and onions in oil, adding more oil if needed. Add mushrooms and broth. Bring to a boil. Add basil and paprika. Cook about 30 minutes until meat is done to taste.

Slowly mix in sour cream until mixture is slightly thickened. This is also a matter of taste. Blend well. Mix in noodles, or serve over hot cooked noodles. Serves 4-6.

Hints: If there seems to be too much liquid before the sour cream is added, use a baster and remove some of the juice, being careful not to remove the basil or vegetables. If the broth is still not beef-tasting enough, add some instant beef bouillon. Serve with a green vegetable. This is an excellent meal!

Put a dried hot pepper in each jar or plastic bag of dried beans or grains to keep away weevils and other insects. A bay leaf will also thwart weevils.

Beef

GROUND BEEF GOULASH

1 lb. lean ground beef
1 tsp. salt
1 dash pepper
3 Tbsp. oil
3 cups medium egg noodles (uncooked)
2 cups water
1 8-oz. can tomato sauce
1 envelope dried onion soup mix

Brown meat in hot oil with salt and pepper, stirring occasionally with
fork, being careful not to break up the meat too much. Drain excess fat.
Sprinkle noodles over cooked meat. Combine all other ingredients and
pour over noodles. Do not stir. Cover and bring to a boil. Reduce heat to
simmer for about 30 minutes, until noodles are tender. Serves 4.

TEX-MEX GRILLED POUCH MEAL

1 1/2 lbs. lean ground round
1 medium onion, diced
4 medium potatoes, cut into bite-size pieces
1 can (12-14 oz.) whole kernel corn, drained
1 package of taco seasoning mix
2 Tbsp. garlic powder
1/2 tsp. course black pepper
4 oz. low-fat (or regular) cheddar cheese, shredded

Mix all ingredients, except cheese, together. Divide mixture into
fourths, and place on four squares of heavy-duty aluminum foil. Seal
securely, and place on grill for 1 hour.

Beef

Open 'pouch' carefully, sprinkle cheese on top, reseal for one minute to let cheese melt. Open up and serve with tortilla chips and picanté sauce.

This can also be done in a traditional oven using a covered glass casserole dish. Bake at 350° for one hour. To lessen cooking time, pre-cook the potatoes in a microwave for three minutes and then chop into bite-size pieces.

SOUTH OF THE BORDER COUSCOUS

1/2 lb. boneless beef sirloin, cut into small thin strips
1 cup frozen corn
1 can black beans, drained, rinsed
1 can fat-free chicken broth
1 can Mexican-style stewed tomatoes, undrained
1 Tbsp. taco seasoning mix
2 tsp. cumin
1 cup uncooked couscous

Spray large nonstick saucepan or Dutch oven with nonstick cooking spray. Heat over medium-high heat until hot. Add beef; cook and stir 3-5 minutes until no longer pink.

Add corn, beans, broth, tomatoes, taco seasoning mix, and cumin. Stir gently to mix. Bring to boil. Reduce heat to medium; cover and cook 5-7 minutes or until vegetables are thoroughly heated.

Stir in couscous. Remove from heat. Cover and let stand 5 minutes or until all liquid is absorbed.

For frequently consumed items such as rice, coffee creamer, sugar, and the like, use smaller containers and place them near the front of a locker. Refill as needed from the less accessible bulk packages.

Beef

BASIC MEAT LOAF

2 pounds lean ground beef (or ground turkey)
1 tsp. salt
1/2 tsp. seasoned salt
1/2 Tbsp. ground black pepper
3 slices bread, soaked in 1/2 cup skim milk
1 large onion, grated
1 clove garlic, minced
2 Tbsp. Worcestershire sauce
3 Tbsp. chili sauce
1 tsp. dry mustard

Preheat oven to 375°. Combine all ingredients and mix well. Pat the
meat mixture into a loaf shape and placed on an oiled, flat baking dish
(easier to slice than when baked in a loaf pan.) Bake 50-60 minutes.
Makes approximately 8 servings.

Option: Top with stewed tomatoes, brown gravy, or bar-b-q sauce.

SWEET AND SOUR MEATBALLS

<u>Meatballs</u>
1 1/2 lbs. lean ground beef
1/2 cup unseasoned bread crumbs
1/2 cup minced onion
1 egg
1/2 tsp. salt
1/8 tsp. pepper
1/3 cup milk
2 Tbsp. oil

Beef

Sauce
2 small cans tomato sauce
1 cup sugar
1/2 cup white vinegar
2-3 shakes Worcestershire sauce
Dash of salt and pepper

Mix all meatball ingredients well. Roll into bite-size balls. Brown in hot oil. Do not remove juices. Add sauce ingredients and stir until well blended. Cover and cook slowly 45 minutes – 1 hour, stirring occasionally. Serves 10-12.

DELICIOUS CORNED BEEF

1 head of cabbage, quartered
2 cans whole new potatoes
1 can corned beef

Put all ingredients in a large pot and heat thoroughly. Simmer 10 minutes and season to taste.

Option: May use ham hocks instead of corned beef.

"Whenever I try a new recipe, I always write: 1) the date; 2) any comments; 3) any ingredients I might have changed or added to make it better; and 4) the place we were when I tried it. Now, looking through my cookbooks brings back some nice memories."

Spray your Tupperware with nonstick cooking spray before pouring in tomato-based sauces. No more stains!

SAUSAGE ROLL

This keeps well for up a month. You can dry it like jerky, and with a time adjustment, it can be made in your pressure cooker.

2 lbs. lean ground beef
2 1/2 Tbsp. Morton Tender Quick Salt*
2 tsp. liquid smoke
1/2 tsp. onion powder
1/4 tsp. garlic powder (or use 2 finely chopped garlic cloves)
1 tsp. mustard seeds
1/8 tsp. pepper
1 cup water

Mix together in a bowl. Roll into two logs and wrap in aluminum foil. Refrigerate 24 hours.

Punch holes in foil along bottom side and bake on a rack in a pan for 1 hour and 15 minutes at 325°.

If using a pressure cooker, pour 1 cup of water in bottom and place on rack, not letting the foil sit in the water. Cook for 8 minutes at 15 pounds pressure, with regulator rocking slowly.

Chill and slice for sandwiches or just use as a snack with crackers and cheese.

- The Tender Quick is essential and there is NO substitute. You can buy it in some stores; you can also order it from The Cumberland General Store in Crossville, Tennessee (1-800-334-4640, www.cumberlandgeneral.com). This company has a wonderful variety of dry stores, spices, herbs, etc.

PORK FRIED RICE

Fried rice is a wonderful way to use leftovers and almost everyone loves it. The trick to fried rice is to always start with COLD rice. Try any of meats and vegetables, cooked ham, shrimp, chicken, turkey, and consider vegetables such as mushrooms, bean sprouts, bamboo shoots, sliced water chestnuts, and even peas and pimiento.

2 eggs
1/4 tsp. salt
4 Tbsp. oil
4 cups COLD rice
1 cup roast pork, diced
2 scallions, sliced
2 Tbsp. soy sauce
1/4 tsp. sugar

Beat eggs and salt very lightly. Heat 1 Tbsp. of oil in a fry pan or wok. Scramble the eggs until they are cooked through, but still moist and fluffy. Remove to a dish.

Heat remaining oil. Add rice and stir-fry 2-3 minutes to coat. Add pork and scallions. Stir-fry until heated through and well mixed. Dissolve sugar in soy sauce and sprinkle over the rice. Add the eggs; toss to break up and mix well with the rice. Serves 4.

Although Chinese cuisine is the inspiration behind stir fries, this technique works well with all cuisines. Try Italian stir fry, using garlic, basil, and balsamic vinegar and serve with pasta instead of rice. For Mexican, use green chilies, coriander, and salsa to make a south-of-the-border dish.

Pork

PORK CHOP & RICE DINNER
Ready in just 20 minutes. Serves 4.

4 pork chops, 3/4 inch thick
1 tsp. poultry seasoning
2 Tbsp. butter or margarine
1 cup sliced celery
1/2 cup chopped onion
2 cups milk
1 can cream of mushroom soup
2 cups Minute Rice, uncooked

Sprinkle pork chops with seasoning. Melt butter in large skillet on
medium-high heat. Add pork chops; cook 5 minutes on each side or until
cooked through. Remove from skillet.

Cook and stir celery and onion in same skillet until tender. Stir in milk
and soup; bring to boil. Stir in rice. Top with pork chops; cover. Cook on
low heat 5 minutes.

SUN-DRIED TOMATO AND SAUSAGE JAMBALAYA MIX

1 cup white basmati rice
5 sun-dried tomatoes (not packed in oil) snipped into small pieces
2 Tbsp. dried soup greens
1/2 chicken bouillon cube, crumbled
1 bay leaf
1/2 tsp. dried oregano
1/2 tsp. paprika
1/2 tsp. salt
1/8 tsp. ground pepper
1/8 tsp. tumeric
Large pinch of cayenne pepper, or more to taste

92

Pork

Pinch of garlic powder
1 oz. hard dried smoked sausage
2 1/2 cups water

At home or at the dock, combine all ingredients, <u>except sausage,</u> in an airtight plastic bag. Seal bag.

When ready to eat, dice sausage. In a medium saucepan, bring water to a boil. Add jambalaya mix and sausage to water and return to a boil. Cover and cook over low heat for about 15 minutes. Remove from heat and let stand for 5 minutes. Fluff with a fork. Serves 2.

Variation: A small tin of smoked mussels can be used instead of sausage.

HAM A LA RAMEN

1-2 packages Ramen (oriental noodle soup)
1/2 cup dried peas
Parmesan cheese to taste
1 5-oz. can ham
Red pepper flakes to taste

Cook the Ramen noodles (without the flavor pack) along with the dried peas. When the noodles are cooked, drain. Top with ham and add red pepper and parmesan cheese to taste. Mix, eat, and enjoy!

Instead of a bulky colander which wastes too much space in the galley locker, buy a handled half-circle of plastic with enough holes to allow easy draining (found at Lechters, Wal-Mart, Target, etc.)

LOW COUNTRY BOIL

New potatoes, 4 per person
Hillshire Polish Sausage, 1/4 lb. per person. Cut into 3" pieces.
Corn on the cob, 1-2 half ears per person
Unpeeled headless shrimp, 1/3 – 1/2 lb. per person
Shrimp or seafood seasoning bag

Put potatoes in water to cover. Boil for 25 minutes. Add sausage and cook 20 minutes. Lift potatoes and sausage out of water onto a pan on top of stove. Add corn to water and cook 7-10 minutes. Remove. Add a shrimp seasoning bag, simmer for 5 minutes, remove, and add shrimp to the boiling water. Cook 3 more minutes or until done. Drain well. Spread on a large platter and top with potatoes, sausage, and corn on the cob. (Hot shrimp will reheat the rest.)

EASY COOKING METHOD: Boil potatoes 20 minutes, add sausage, and cook 10 more minutes. Add corn and cook 7 minutes. Then add shrimp and boil 3 minutes. Drain well. Everything is boiled together and no shrimp seasoning is added.

Make sausage broiling easy by pressing several links onto a meat skewer—one flip turns them all.

Flouring sausage patties on both sides gives them an appetizing, crunchy crust as they fry. This method also helps prevent splattering.

Learn from labels: Regular smoked link sausage can contain as much as 8 grams of fat per ounce! Some brands of reduced fat smoked link sausage have 4 grams per ounce. On occasion you can find even "healthier" brands that only contain 1 gram per ounce.

GRILLED SALMON IN A BAG
1 salmon fillet (about 1 1/2 lb.)
3 Tbsp. balsamic vinegar
1 1/2 Tbsp. chopped garlic
1/2 tsp. onion powder
1/8 tsp. garlic salt
1 Tbsp. chopped chives
2 Tbsp. mustard seeds
Olive oil (Will vary, depending upon your taste. I use about 6-8 tablespoons.)
Black pepper
Parsley
1 large piece of aluminum foil or 1 medium foil bag

Place salmon fillet in foil bag. If you don't have the bag, a large piece of aluminum foil will do just fine. Mix vinegar, garlic, onion powder, chives, mustard seeds, and olive oil; drizzle mixture over fillet. Top with black pepper and parsley. Wrap up salmon tightly in foil bag or foil sheet. Place in a preheated grill, medium-low. Grill for approximately 20-25 minutes and use tongs to turn the bag often. (Remember that grills do vary in temperatures.) Take off grill; BE CAREFUL, the bag is extremely hot! Place on tray and serve hot or cold.

Baking fish on a bed of chopped onion, celery, and parsley not only makes the fish taste better, but also keeps it from sticking to the pan.

To remove fish odor from hands, rub them with vinegar or salt.

To rid frying pans of fish odor, sprinkle salt in the pan, add hot water, and allow to stand awhile before rinsing.

BASIL-BUTTERED SALMON STEAKS
Ready in 15 minutes. Serves 4.

1/2 cup butter or margarine
1 Tbsp. snipped fresh basil
1 Tbsp. snipped parsley
1/8 tsp. pepper
2 tsp. lemon juice
4 salmon fillets, about 2 lbs. (You can substitute swordfish, shark, or halibut steaks.)

Mix butter, basil, parsley, and lemon juice in a small bowl. Place fish on the greased rack on an unheated broiler pan. Lightly brush fish with some of the butter mixture. Broil 4 inches from the heat for 5 minutes. Then, using a wide spatula, carefully turn fish over. Lightly brush with more of the butter mixture.

Broil for 3-7 minutes or until fish is done. To serve, dollop remaining butter mixture on top of fish.

To grill: Prepare steaks as directed above, except brush grill rack with cooking oil.

Place fish on rack. Lightly brush fish with butter mixture. Grill fish on an uncovered grill directly over medium-hot coals for 5 minutes.

Carefully turn fish over. Lightly brush with more butter mixture and grill for 3-7 minutes more or until fish is done. Dollop remaining butter mixture on top of fish.

Good accompaniments include steamed green beans, basmati rice, or rice pilaf.

GARLIC SHRIMP AND PASTA

2 Tbsp. cornstarch
1 can chicken broth
2 cloves garlic, minced
3 Tbsp. chopped fresh parsley, or 1 Tbsp. dried parsley flakes
2 Tbsp. lemon juice
1/8 Tbsp. ground red pepper
1 pound medium shrimp, shelled and deveined
4 cups hot cooked thin spaghetti (about 8 oz. dry)

In medium saucepan, mix cornstarch, broth, garlic, lemon juice, and pepper. Over medium-high heat, cook until mixture boils and thickens, stirring constantly.

Add shrimp. Cook 5 minutes or until shrimp turn pink, stirring often. Toss with spaghetti. If desired, garnish with lime.

You can substitute diced chicken for the shrimp, if you prefer. Delicious!

After shelling and deveining shrimp, put them in a bowl and wash gently under cold, running water for half a minute. Next, rinse them in a colander under running water for another three minutes. When cooked, they will almost crunch.

Canned shrimp lose their "canned taste" if you soak them for 15 minutes in two tablespoons of vinegar and a teaspoon of sherry.

To determine how much shrimp to buy: If unpeeled, 1/3-1/2 lb. per person. Peeled shrimp, 1/4-1/3 lb. per person.

CITRUS SHRIMP

1 pound of peeled, deveined shrimp
1/2 cup prepared citrus sauce (i.e. McCormick Flavor Medleys lemon
pepper sauce)
1 cup snow peas
1 red bell pepper, cut into strips
4 cups hot cooked rice

Combine shrimp, peas, bell pepper, and sauce in a 2-quart casserole.
Cover with lid or vented plastic wrap. Stirring midway through cooking,
microwave on high 4-5 minutes or until shrimp turn pink and vegetables
are crisp tender. Serve over rice.

SHRIMP WITH CURRIED COUSCOUS

2 tsp. olive oil
2 garlic cloves, minced
3/4 lb. shrimp; shelled, deveined, uncooked
2 medium onions, chopped
2 tsp. curry powder
1 9-oz. package frozen mixed vegetables, thawed
1 14.5-oz. can stewed tomatoes, undrained
1 cup chicken broth
1 cup uncooked couscous

Heat oil in medium nonstick skillet or large saucepan over medium-high
heat. Add garlic; cook and stir 30 seconds or until golden brown.

Add shrimp; cook and stir 2-3 minutes or until shrimp turn pink. Using
slotted spoon, remove shrimp from skillet; place in small bowl. Cover to
keep warm.

Add onions and curry powder to skillet; mix well. Stir in veggies. Cover; cook 5-7 minutes or until onions are tender, stirring occasionally.

Stir in tomatoes and broth. Cover; bring to boil. Stir in couscous and shrimp. Remove from heat; cover and let stand 5-6 minutes or until all liquid is absorbed.

SCALLOP AND SHRIMP KABOBS

1 lb. sea scallops, cleaned
1 lb. shrimp, peeled and deveined
1 Tbsp. fresh cilantro, chopped
3 cloves garlic, minced
1/2 - 3/4 cup orange juice
1 Tbsp. brandy
Vegetables of your choice

Marinate in a Ziploc bag for 15 minutes. Thread on skewers. Grill or broil until shrimp turns pink. Baste occasionally.

QUICK RICH LOBSTER

1 1/2 - 2 lbs. cooked lobster meat, cut into good-sized chunks
1/2 lb. butter
8 oz. chili sauce
Few sprinkles of Worcestershire sauce
1/4 cup sherry

Melt butter in a good size saucepan. Add chili sauce. Heat, mixing well. Add Worcestershire sauce to taste. Add sherry. Add lobster meat and heat to serving temperature. Serve over toast points. Serves 4.

EGGS DUNGENESS

2 large fresh Dungeness crabs (not canned!)
1/4 cup Old Bay seasoning
Fresh chives
Parsley
Olives
Sweet peppers, chopped
4 English muffins, halved
4 eggs

Hollandaise sauce
4 egg yolks
2 Tbsp. lemon juice
1/4 tsp. white or cayenne pepper
1/2 lb. unsalted butter, melted
1 Tbsp. hot water
2 egg whites

Boil crab with Old Bay seasoning. Cool and clean. This may be done the night before.

To make the sauce, combine yolks, lemon juice, and pepper with a wire whisk in the top of a double boiler; slowly whisk in butter. Add hot water to help stabilize the sauce. Remove from heat. In a separate bowl, beat egg whites until very stiff. With a wire whisk, gently fold egg whites into sauce.

Toast English muffin halves very lightly. Poach eggs. Warm crab meat and place a healthy amount on each English muffin half. Top crab with poached egg and lace with sauce. Garnish with fresh chives, parsley, olives, or chopped peppers. Makes 4 servings.

WEST INDIES CRAB

1/4 cup olive oil
1 1/4 tsp. salt
3 Tbsp. wine vinegar
1/4 tsp. dry mustard
1/4 Tbsp. black pepper
Dash of ground thyme
1/4 tsp. dried basil leaves
1 Tbsp. minced fresh parsley
1 1/4 cup coarsely chopped onion
1/8 tsp. sugar
2 Tbsp. lime juice
1 lb. crab

Mix all ingredients, except crab. Then add the crab and toss. Pack mixture gently and refrigerate at least 4 hours. Re-toss at intervals.

EASY AND DELICIOUS FISH

Fish fillets
Mayonnaise
Lemon juice
Parmesan cheese
Salt and pepper
Paprika

Wash fish and pat dry. Line baking dish with foil. Place fish in pan, skin side down. Sprinkle generously with salt and pepper. Spread mayonnaise evenly over fish, including edges. Sprinkle lightly with Parmesan cheese and paprika. Bake for 15-20 minutes in 450° oven, or until done. Place under broiler for 1 minute until lightly browned and puffed.

OYSTER ROCKEFELLER CASSEROLE

1 qt. raw oysters
1 stick butter
1 rib celery, fine chopped
1 medium onion, finely chopped
1/2 cup parsley, finely chopped
1 box frozen chopped spinach, thawed and drained
1/2 tsp. anise seed
1/4 cup Worcestershire sauce
1/2 cup breadcrumbs
1 cup sharp cheese, grated
Breadcrumbs
Salt, pepper, and cayenne to taste

Drain oysters. Melt butter and sauté celery. Add onions, parsley, spinach, anise seed, Worcestershire sauce, breadcrumbs, salt, pepper, and cayenne.

Grease a shallow casserole. Arrange oysters in one layer only. Cover with Rockefeller mixture as thick as desired. Bake in 450° oven for 30 minutes. Remove and sprinkle with grated cheese and a very thin layer of breadcrumbs. Return to oven for 10 minutes until slightly brown.

Buy an assortment of odd measuring cups at thrift shops. Put them in your containers to measure without having to pull out the set of measuring cups.

Are your paper towels being unfurled by the breeze blowing through your galley? A hat/corsage pin stuck through the paper will control them. Painting the head of the pin with fingernail polish will make it much more visible.

Seafood

CURRIED RICE & TUNA

2 cups instant rice
1/2 tsp. salt
1/2 cup seedless raisins
1 6-oz. can tuna in water, drained. Reserve liquid.
4 cups water
2 tsp. margarine
2 tsp. curry powder
1 hard boiled egg, chopped

Cook the rice according to the package directions, using the water, salt, and margarine. While rice is cooking, peel the hard-boiled egg and finely chop. Drain most of the water from the tuna. When the rice is cooked, leave over low flame and toss the raisins, curry, egg, and tuna with a small amount of tuna water. Mix thoroughly and heat briefly. Remove from heat and serve. A couple of tablespoons of chopped almonds makes a good addition to this recipe.

FIVE CAN TUNA CASSEROLE
Hardly a gourmet meal, but does well in a pinch!

1 can tuna
1 can peas
1 can chicken noodle soup
1 small can mushrooms
1 can Durkee's onions (use half in mixture and half on top to serve)

Mix all ingredients together and place in a greased casserole to bake at 350° for 30 minutes, or heat on top of stove. Serves 4.

TEX-MEX TUNA SALAD

1 lb. tuna, cooked and cubed
1/4 cup lime juice
1 jalapeno pepper, minced
2 cucumbers, cubed
2 cups fresh cilantro, minced
Salt and pepper to taste

Combine and serve on beds of romaine lettuce. Garnish with lime wedges
and salsa.

THE PERFECT TUNA CASSEROLE

1 can cream of mushroom soup
1/3 cup milk
6 1/2 oz. tuna; drained and flaked
2 eggs; hard boiled, sliced
1 cup peas, cooked
1 cup potato chips

Preheat oven to 350°. Slightly crumble the potato chips. Blend soup and
milk in 1-quart casserole. Stir in tuna, eggs, and peas. Bake 20 minutes.
Top with chips; bake 10 minutes longer.

Add a few tablespoons of milk when reheating tuna casseroles for a
creamy consistency.

If you are prone to nicking your fingers when grating cheese, try
covering 2 or 3 of them with metal thimbles. You'll be able to grate
faster and closer.

CHICKEN PAPRIKAS

1 chicken, cup into pieces (approx. 3 lbs.)
Salt and pepper
2-4 Tbsp. vegetable oil
1 onion, chopped
1 green pepper, chopped
5 cloves garlic, minced
1/4 cup tomato sauce
2 Tbsp. paprika
3 Tbsp. dill weed
1 cup chicken broth
1 Tbsp. flour
3/4 cup sour cream

Sprinkle chicken with salt and pepper. Heat oil in a 4- or 6-quart pressure cooker. Sauté onions, green pepper, and garlic until tender; remove. Brown chicken a few pieces at a time; set aside.

Add tomato sauce, paprika, dill weed, and a small amount of chicken broth to oil in pressure cooker; stir until smooth. Add remaining broth, stirring to mix. Return chicken and vegetables to pressure cooker. Close pressure cooker cover securely. Place pressure regulator on vent pipe. Cook for 8 minutes at 15 pounds pressure, with regulator rocking slowly. Cool pressure cooker at once. Remove chicken and vegetables to a warm dish. Stir flour into sour cream; add to hot liquid. Cook and stir until mixture simmers and thickens. Pour sauce over chicken. Makes 4-6 servings.

One of the most important accessories you will need is a timer. A couple of extra minutes of cooking probably won't harm a pot roast, but it could ruin a more delicate dish or any accompanying veggies.

SOPA MAGICA

1 chicken, cut into pieces
13 garlic cloves
1 bay leaf
2 tsp. salt
6 cups water
1 orange, grate rind and juice
2 Tbsp. fresh cilantro

Put ingredients in a pressure cooker. Pressure cook at high for 20 minutes. Turn the heat off, allow to cool naturally. Strain and discard the onion, garlic, and bay leaf. Transfer the broth to a bowl and refrigerate so you then skim off and discard all the fat. Refrigerate the chicken. When ready to eat, discard chicken skin and bones and shred the meat. Transfer the broth to a heavy pot and bring to a boil. Lower the heat, add the shredded chicken, and stir for about 1 minute. Add the grated orange rind and orange juice; stir. Garnish with cilantro.

BRUNSWICK STEW

2 1/2 lb. chicken, cut into serving pieces (remove skin)
Flour for dredging
4 slices bacon, fried and crumbled[1] (reserve fat for browning chicken)
1 tsp. each: salt, pepper, sugar, dried tarragon
1 can lima beans, drained
1 can corn kernels, drained
1 cup large diced potatoes
1 recipe dumplings or package Gnocchi[2], cooked according to package directions

Dredge chicken in flour; cook bacon in rendered bacon fat or vegetable oil. Place all ingredients, except dumplings, in order given. Close cover

106

securely. Place regulator on vent and cook 20 minutes with regulator rocking slowly. Cool cooker at once (running under cold water, avoiding getting water in covered vent.)

Add gnocchi or add dumpling dough to simmering stew at this point. Stew becomes thicker with homemade dumplings, so if using gnocchi, you may wish to thicken a little.

[1] Bacon fat adds flavor. However, oil may be used to brown chicken without compromising much.

[2] Gnocchi is an Italian dumpling available in many supermarkets, specialty shops, and Costco. Does not require refrigeration until opened. It can be served with a variety of sauces, in soups, or in stews.

Cut same foods into pieces of uniform size to promote even cooking. When mixing foods, cut those that cook more quickly into larger pieces and those that cook more slowly into smaller pieces.

Once you have reduced pressure according to directions, shake the pot before opening the seal to readjust the inner temperature.

When storing your pressure cooker, be sure to store it with the lid completely detached and to the side of the pot. If you store it closed, you will trap smells and odors inside the pot to greet you on your next usage. Thoroughly wash the rubber seal and rub it with mineral oil after each use to preserve it. The rubber seal should last through about 150 meals. Store the valve and rubber seal (if not attached) inside the cooker.

SWEET 'N SOUR CHICKEN

1 chicken cut up (approx. 3 lbs.)
1 Tbsp. vegetable or olive oil
1/2 cup sliced celery
1 green or red pepper, cut into chunks
1 20-oz. can pineapple chunks, drained and juice reserved
1 cup reserved pineapple juice (add water if necessary)
1/4 cup brown sugar
1/2 cup vinegar
2 Tbsp. soy sauce
1 Tbsp. ketchup
1/2 tsp. Worcestershire sauce
1/4 tsp. ground ginger
2 Tbsp. cornstarch
2 Tbsp. cold water

Heat oil in a 4- or 6-quart pressure cooker. Brown chicken a few pieces at a time; set aside. Return all chicken to pressure cooker; add celery and green pepper. Combine pineapple juice, brown sugar, vinegar, soy sauce, ketchup, Worcestershire sauce, and ginger. Pour over chicken.

Close pressure cooker securely. Place pressure regulator on vent pipe. Cook for 8 minutes at 15 pounds pressure, with regulator rocking slowly. Cool pressure cooker at once. Remove chicken and vegetables to a warm platter.

Mix cornstarch with cold water; blend into hot liquid. Cook and stir until mixture boils and thickens. Add pineapple chunks and heat. Pour sauce over chicken. Serve with rice. Makes 4-6 servings.

The first commercial pressure cooker debuted in the United States at the New York World's Fair in 1939.

SAILOR'S MASH

1 can roast beef (or fresh stewing beef*)
8 slices bacon, cut into small pieces
1 onion, diced
1 tsp. each: dill, salt, thyme
1/2 tsp. pepper
1 cup water
6 potatoes, cubed (leave skin on)
4 carrots, sliced

Put bacon, onion, potatoes, and carrots into cooker. Add spices. Pour water on top. Don't stir (this keeps the bacon on the bottom of the cooker.) Add beef (do not drain.) Pressure cook for 6 minutes after first jiggle. Stir well. Serve with bread.

* If using fresh beef, you may wish to brown the beef and bacon together first.

Helpful accessories for your pressure cooker include: a rack or trivot, which commonly comes with the cooker; a steamer basket to keep foods above the liquid is also desirable for cooking some vegetables. To cook desserts you will need a 5-cup heatproof soufflé dish (that fits in side your pressure cooker); 1/2-cup heatproof ramekins for puddings, custards and timbales; and a 7- or 8-inch springform pan (to fit in your cooker) for cheesecakes. You should also have a heat-diffuser, which prevents direct contact between the heat source and the bottom of the cooker. It comes in handy when preparing rice, pasta or bean dishes to prevent sticking and scorching.

EASY, SPICY MEXICAN RICE

1 cup uncooked white rice (do not use instant!)
1 can kidney beans; do not drain
1 can chicken; drain and reserve liquid in measuring cup
1 can stewed tomatoes or Rotel with green chilies (drain and reserve liquid in measuring cup)
2 heaping tsp. chili powder
3 tsp. dried oregano
1 tsp. ground thyme
2 (or more) smashed garlic cloves
1 onion, chopped
2 chicken bouillon cubes (or 1 tsp. salt if you prefer)
Water

Drain liquid from canned chicken and tomatoes into measuring cup. Add water to liquids to equal 2 cups total. Place all ingredients in pressure cooker and stir. Cover and bring up to pressure. Cook 4 minutes. Let the pressure drop on its own. Serve as a main dish with grated cheddar cheese and sour cream. Delicious!

CORNED BEEF

3 pounds corned beef
2 cups water
1 Tbsp. garlic powder
1 bay leaf

Pour 2 cups water into cooker. Position steamer basket in cooker. Rub garlic powder into all surfaces of corned beef. Place corned beef in steamer basket. Add bay leaf. Close cover securely. Place pressure regulator on vent pipe and cook 60 minutes at 15 pounds pressure, with pressure regulator rocking slowly. Let pressure drop of its own accord.

For Your Sweet Tooth

EASY PEANUT BUTTER COOKIES

1 14-oz. can Eagle Brand sweetened condensed milk
3/4 cup peanut butter
2 cups Bisquick
1 tsp. vanilla
Sugar

Preheat oven to 375°. In large mixing bowl, beat milk and peanut butter until smooth. Add Bisquick and vanilla. Mix well. Shape into 1" balls. Roll each ball in sugar. Place 2 inches apart on ungreased cookie sheet. Flatten with fork. Bake 6-8 minutes, or until lightly brown. Resist temptation to over-bake. Cool. Store tightly covered.

WORLD'S BEST CHOCOLATE CHIP COOKIES

Cream:
1 1/2 cups butter or margarine (3 sticks, softened)
1 cup sugar
1 1/4 cups packed light brown sugar
1 Tbsp. vanilla
2 eggs

Mix:
4 cups all-purpose flour
2 tsp. baking soda
1 tsp. salt
1 24-oz. package milk chocolate chips
Optional: 1 cup nuts, chopped (pecans, walnuts work well)

Add dry ingredients to creamed mixture. Drop by rounded spoonfuls onto greased cookie sheet. Bake at 350° for 12-15 minutes. Allow to cool on rack. Makes 5 1/2 dozen cookies.

NO BAKE COOKIES

2 cups sugar
1/2 cup cocoa
1/2 cup peanut butter
1/2 cup milk
1/2 cup butter
1tsp. vanilla
3 cups quick oats

Mix sugar, cocoa, peanut butter, milk, and butter in a pan. Over a
medium heat and watching carefully, bring to full boil; boil for one
minute, stirring often. Remove from heat. Stir in oats and then add
vanilla. Drop spoonfuls onto waxed paper and let cool until hardened.

CREAM CHEESE BROWNIES

1 box German chocolate cake mix
1 8-oz. package cream cheese, softened
1 egg
1/2 cup sugar
1/2 cup milk chocolate chips

Mix cake mix according to directions. In separate bowl, mix cream
cheese, egg, sugar, and chips (with mixer.) Pour cake batter into pan.
Drop cream cheese mixture by spoonfuls on top of batter. Using a knife,
make swirls so that cream cheese mixture is evenly spread throughout
batter. Bake according to directions on box.

For bread recipes calling for use of a <u>dough hook</u>: lightly oil the hook
before kneading your bread. The oil will keep the dough from "climbing"
and will make cleaning up easier.

SUGAR-DUSTED MOCHA BROWNIES

This light, yet fudgy version of an all-time favorite features a touch of coffee and a pretty powdered-sugar top.

1/2 cup all-purpose flour
1/2 cup unsweetened cocoa powder
1/2 tsp. baking powder
4 Tbsp. light margarine (1/4 cup)
1 Tbsp. instant coffee crystals
1 cup sugar
2 eggs
1/4 cup prune baby food
2 tsp. vanilla
Vegetable oil spray
2 Tbsp. powdered sugar

Pre-heat oven to 350°. In a small bowl, combine flour, cocoa powder, and baking powder. Set aside.

In a medium saucepan, melt margarine. Add coffee crystals and stir until dissolved. Remove from heat and cool slightly. Using a wooden spoon, add sugar, eggs, prune baby food, and vanilla to coffee mixture. Stir until well combined. Fold cocoa mixture into sugar mixture until well combined.

Spray 8" x 8" x 2" cake pan with vegetable oil spray. Spoon batter into pan. Bake, uncovered, for 18-20 minutes, or until a toothpick inserted near the center comes out almost clean (it should have a few fudgy crumbs on it.)

Cool brownies in the pan on a wire rack. Sift powdered sugar over the brownies.

For Your Sweet Tooth

SIMPLE PINEAPPLE CAKE

5 egg whites
1 20-oz. can crushed pineapple, not drained
1 reduced-fat yellow cake mix
Topping: 1 Tbsp. sugar

Beat egg whites with electric mixer until foamy. Add pineapple and the
dry cake mix. Mix. Spread in a sprayed and floured 9" x 13" pan.
Sprinkle with sugar. Bake at 350° for 35 minutes or until done.

ROOSTER CAKE
No eggs!

3/4 cup sugar
1 1/2 cups flour
1/3 - 1/2 cup cocoa
1 tsp. baking soda
1/2 cup oil
1 cup cold water
2 Tbsp. vinegar

Whisk together first six ingredients. Add vinegar and stir. Pre-heat
oven to 375° for 25 minutes or until done.

May be cooked in the microwave for 5 minutes at 50% power, turning 2-3
times, then a couple of more minutes on full power.

When a recipe calls for chocolate slivers, you can make the finest
shavings of chocolate yourself. A chocolate bar and a potato peeler will
do the trick cheaply and conveniently.

For Your Sweet Tooth

YOGURT PIE

1 graham cracker crust
1 carton strawberry yogurt
1 small package strawberry Jell-O
Fresh or frozen strawberries
Cool Whip

Boil 1 1/4 cups water. Add Jell-O and stir well until dissolved.
Mix Jell-O into the yogurt; stir until mixed well. Pour into crust.
Refrigerate until set. Top with fresh berries and Cool Whip.

LIGHT KEY LIME PIE

1 8 oz. carton fat-free Cool Whip
1 graham cracker pie crust
1 can fat-free sweetened condensed milk
1/3 cup key lime juice

Mix Cool Whip, milk, and lime juice. Pour into prepared pie crust and
refrigerate several hours.

Cool baked goods in draft-free places because drafts tend to cause
shrinkage.

To cut down on cholesterol, for each whole egg called for in a recipe,
substitute two egg whites stiffly beaten and folded into the cake
batter.

MARLBOROUGH PIE

This is a New England recipe. The rich yellow pie has a sharp lemon
taste with the texture of apple custard.

Unbaked 9" pie shell
1 cup unsweetened applesauce
3 Tbsp. lemon juice
1/2 tsp. lemon peel
3/4 cup sugar
4 eggs, slightly beaten
2 Tbsp. melted butter
1/2 tsp. salt

Chill the pie shell while preparing the filling. Combine the remaining
ingredients. Blend thoroughly and pour into chilled pie shell. Bake at
450° degrees for 15 minutes. Reduce the heat to 350° and bake 10-15
minutes longer, or until a silver knife inserted halfway between the
center and edge of the pie comes out clean. Cool on a rack. If you feel
really decadent, serve with whipped cream on top.

Next time you make an apple pie, add flavor by sprinkling a cup of
coconut over the apples before covering them with the top crust.

When measuring oil and honey for a recipe, measure the oil first so that
it coats the spoon or cup, making the honey that's measured next slide
out easily.

Don't keep baking power for more than one year, as it loses its potency.
To check whether your baking powder is still good, add one teaspoon of
it to 1/3 cup of hot tap water. The mixture should bubble vigorously.

For Your Sweet Tooth

PEANUT BUTTER CHEESECAKE
This recipe is to die for! And not too sweet.

1 3-oz. package cream cheese
1 cup powdered sugar
1/4 cup milk
1 cup chunk-style peanut butter (or your favorite style)
2 tsp. vanilla
1 1/2 cups whipping cream
1 already-prepared pie crust

Whip cream cheese and sugar until fluffy. Beat in milk, peanut butter, and vanilla. In a chilled bowl, beat whipping cream until stiff. Stir 1/3 of the whipping cream into the peanut butter mixture. Fold in the remaining whipping cream. Pour the entire mixture into pie crust and let stand in the freezer for 2-3 hours. Remove from freezer to thaw about half an hour before serving.

TAFFY APPLE DESSERT
This tastes just like a taffy apple, but without the mess on your face!

Freeze 6 Snickers candy bars.   Then place in a Zip-loc bag and break them into small, bite-size piece, using a hammer or mallet.

Toss the following ingredients together right before serving:

6 Granny Smith apples, cut into 1" bites
1 small container of Light Cool Whip
The frozen Snicker's bites

(Note: This recipe does not keep very well for very long. Eat soon after making.)

PROVISIONING
It's Easier Than You Think!

1. VOW TO MAKE A FRESH START
    a. Empty all cabinets and cubbies.
        i. Sort items by category: canned vegetables, soups, snacks, condiments, canned meats, etc.
    b. Clean cabinets and cubbies using your favorite cleaner.
        i. Or make your own all-purpose cleaner by combining <u>1/4 cup baking soda, 1/2 cup white vinegar, 3/4 cup household ammonia, and 1 gallon warm water</u>. Allow to dry thoroughly.
        ii. Now is a good time to also wipe off all the cans and bottles that were stored.
    c. Position any pest-repellents, such as bay leaves, roach cookies*, etc., inside cabinets and cubbies.
        i. To make roach cookies, <u>mix boric acid with a little bacon grease</u>. The mixture should be similar to the consistency of biscuit dough. If it's runny, add a little <u>flour</u>.
        ii. More recipes for pest-repellents can be found in "The Best Tips from Women Aboard." Ordering information, p. 127.
    d. If desired, line cabinets and cubbies with nonskid liner or the liner of your choice.

2. MAKE A LIST OF ALL YOUR FAVORITE MEALS
    a. Think in terms of "meals," i.e. breakfasts, lunches, dinners, snacks.
        i. What might help you think: Save <u>grocery receipts</u> for at least a month or two. This will tell you exactly what you what you are inclined to buy.
        ii. Take a look at all the items you pulled out of the cabinets and cubbies. Given these items to begin with, what can be made?
            1. Lots of canned tuna? What will you need to make your favorite tuna

PROVISIONING
It's Easier Than You Think!

salad? Mayonnaise, celery, perhaps some lemon juice...and don't forget the bread or crackers!
   b. Make a list of a week's worth of meals, 3 meals/day
        i. Even better, plan 2 weeks!
   c. Make a chart similar to that shown below:

	Breakfast	Lunch	Dinner	Snacks
SUN	Eggs Benedict	Sandwiches	Meatloaf, mashed potatoes	Popcorn, fruit
MON	Cereal	Leftovers; if none, sandwiches	Chicken pot pie	Cheese and crackers
TUES	Yogurt, bagels	Hamburgers	Spaghetti, salad	Fruit, cookies
WED	Cinnamon rolls	Ramen noodles, veggie sticks	Grilled fish, vegetables	Rice cakes
THURS	Cereal	Soup and salad	Chicken stroganoff	Fruit and cheese
FRI	French toast	Sandwiches	Pizza	Veggie dip, veggies
SAT	Pancakes	Leftovers; if none, sandwich	Fried rice with seafood	Egg rolls

3. MAKE A LIST of every ingredient necessary to prepare the meals on your chart.
    a. List everything. If "salad" is on your list, remember to list croutons, bacon bits, salad dressing, etc.
    b. Include accompaniments, drinks, condiments, etc.
    c. Remember to include items such as toothpicks, straws, birthday candles, health & beauty products, etc.

4. CROSS OFF THE LIST items that you currently have on board.

PROVISIONING
It's Easier Than You Think!

5. What you are left with is your SHOPPING LIST!
    a. Get real: Buy products and foods you already eat.
    b. Special occasions are even <u>more special</u> on a boat, so make sure you include items such as cake mixes, candles, champagne, etc.
    c. Be prepared for problem times and emergencies. Stock up on items that are quick to prepare and are <u>satisfying</u>.
    d. If you will be traveling far from home, <u>stock up on things you love</u> (Oreos, candy bars, etc.) When you crave them, you'll be glad you have them!

6. When you return from the grocery store:
    a. SORT your purchases according to the categories you have already determined (1ai).
    b. PLAN YOUR STORAGE. <u>Draw a layout of your boat</u> and include every cabinet and cubby.
    c. Assign a meaningful CODE for every cabinet and cubby. One easy method:
        i. Assign "P" for those located on the port side of the boat; "S" for those on the starboard side of the boat.
        ii. Assign a number to each "P" and "S" cabinet and cubby. Start with 1. You'll end up with a layout of all available storage areas, labeled P1, P2, P3, etc., for those on the port side; and S1, S2, S3, etc., for cabinets/cubbies on the starboard side of the boat.

7. STORE YOUR PROVISIONS
    a. Items purchased in bulk can be divided into smaller, easier-to-use portions. Refill as needed.
    b. Keep weight in mind. The heavier the item, the lower it should be stored.

PROVISIONING
It's Easier Than You Think!

c. Remember to <u>divide and conquer!</u>
  i. Use plastic bins to contain like-items, such as condiments.
  ii. Use a dishwashing pan to hold bottled items.
    1. It will contain the bottles, and should a bottle break, the plastic pan will contain the mess!

8. When you are satisfied with how and where you have stored everything, MAKE A LIST.
  a. Use the format in 6C as a guide. List everything that is in P1, P2, and so on. Also list quantities of each item.
  b. Keep this list in a special notebook.
    i. Plastic sheets can contain individual pages, which can then be stored in a binder.
      1. Makes it easy to keep updated.

9. This is your MASTER INVENTORY.
  a. Congratulations! In addition to having the ingredients for 21+ meals, you know where everything is, and where specific items can be found!
  b. It is up to you whether or not you keep track of every single item you use. Some people are very meticulous about keeping track; but if this is the method-of-choice, EVERYONE on the boat needs to keep track.

10. This method can be used to keep track of everything else on board, such as TOOLS, SPARE PARTS, CLOTHING, etc.

Imagine how good you'll feel when you can retrieve that spare fuel filter when you need it, or that nice, warm throw when the temperatures suddenly dip. Take the time to organize and inventory; you (and everyone else on the boat) will be glad you did!

INDEX OF RECIPES

INDEX OF RECIPES

INDEX OF TIPS

INDEX OF TIPS